A SENSE OF HIS PRESENCE

Other books by John Killinger:

HEMINGWAY AND THE DEAD GODS

THE FAILURE OF THEOLOGY IN MODERN LITERATURE

THE CENTRALITY OF PREACHING IN THE TOTAL TASK
OF THE MINISTRY

FOR GOD'S SAKE, BE HUMAN

WORLD IN COLLAPSE: THE VISION OF ABSURD DRAMA

LEAVE IT TO THE SPIRIT: FREEDOM AND COMMITMENT
IN THE NEW LITURGY

THE SALVATION TREE

ALL YOU LONELY PEOPLE, ALL YOU LOVELY PEOPLE

THE FRAGILE PRESENCE: TRANSCENDENCE IN MODERN LITERATURE

EXPERIMENTAL PREACHING

THE SECOND COMING OF THE CHURCH

THE 11:00 O'CLOCK NEWS AND OTHER EXPERIMENTAL SERMONS

BREAD FOR THE WILDERNESS, WINE FOR THE JOURNEY:
THE MIRACLE OF PRAYER AND MEDITATION

THE WORD NOT BOUND: A ONE-ACT PLAY

The Devotional Commentary: Matthew

A SENSE OF HIS PRESENCE

by John Killinger

Drawings by Andy Bacon

DOUBLEDAY AND COMPANY, INC.
GARDEN CITY, NEW YORK
1977

The author and publisher express their appreciation to the following for permission to include the material indicated:

Scripture from the *Revised Standard Version of the Bible*, Copyright 1946, 1952, © 1971, 1973 by the National Council of the Churches of Christ in the U.S.A.

Scripture from J. B. Phillips: *The New Testament in Modern English*, Revised Edition, Copyright © 1958, 1960, 1972 by J. B. Phillips.

Scripture from *The New English Bible*, Copyright © by The Delegates of the Oxford University Press and The Syndics of the Cambridge University Press 1961, 1970. Reprinted by permission.

Library of Congress Cataloging in Publication Data
Killinger, John.
    A sense of His presence.

    (The Devotional commentary: Matthew)
      1. Bible. N. T. Matthew—Devotional literature.
I. Title. II. Series.
BS2575.4.K54   225'.2'06
  ISBN 0-385-12715-4
Library of Congress Catalog Card Number 77–1038

Contents

Introduction

The Gospel of Matthew, like the other Gospels, was written primarily for the Christian community, not as an evangelical tract to convert outsiders to the faith. Its purpose was to help Christians understand more about the life and teachings of the Lord to whom they had pledged their lives, so that they might in turn live as better stewards of God's grace.

It is for this reason, more than any other, that we continue to read the Gospel in our own day.

The Gospel of Matthew, to be sure, does have historical interest for us. It shows us more clearly than the other Gospels how much of Jesus' ministry was shaped by his persistent conflict with the Pharisees, who were concerned for the careful preservation of the Law of Moses and its many addenda. It abounds in comparisons between the old Law and the teachings of Jesus, demonstrating that Christianity, not the Judaism of the scribes and Pharisees, fulfilled the spirit of Moses. It indicates more extensively than the other Gospels that the relationship between Jesus and the disciples was that of teacher and students, and that many of the sayings which we would otherwise assume were broadcast to the crowds were in actuality given only to the disciples, who in turn became the teachers of the crowds. And it delineates, as the other Gospels do not, the special relationship between Jesus and Peter, who became the main leader of the early church, and whose failures as a disciple would have been all the more important as moral lessons to other members of the Christian community.

But it is to learn how *we* can be more faithful in our discipleship today that we still read the Gospel of Matthew. We read it in order to bring our vision of Christ into sharper focus, and to hear his instructions in clearer terms for our own lives and ministries.

For this reason, a devotional commentary on the Gospel may

be even more important to us than a scholarly commentary. It is not intended to supplant scholarly commentaries, which are of inestimable value in their own way. Rather, it attempts in tone and emphasis to bring the reader into keener awareness of a presence —the presence of the living Christ and the absolute presence of God—in a manner totally outside the intention of scholarly compositions. It combines, as fully as possible within the limits of space, the finest fruits of recent scholarship with the devotional stance of the man or woman at prayer. It aims at knowledge; but, more than that, at dedication.

It is not extrinsic to the purpose of this volume, then, to say a word about how it might best be read.

First, it should be read *with* the Gospel of Matthew. It is not a substitute for the reading of the Word itself, but a companion book, a prompter of thoughts the reader may not have had on his or her own while reading the scripture.

Then, as the book is intended to increase the measure of the reader's devotion, each segment should be read quietly, meditatively, in a spirit of listening prayer. As in eating, no more should be ingested at a sitting than can be digested or properly reflected upon. The aim should not be to complete the reading of the book in order to say, "There, that is that," but to live with it as a companion for as long as it continues to guide you into closer association with the One who is its unfailing subject.

This much is certain: We cannot live day by day with the thoughts of the Gospels and not be changed. It is like living in the mountains or living by the sea: gradually and inexplicably, our personalities become altered, are elevated, assuming the character of their environment.

So, I trust, it will be with you as you make your way through this volume.

Nashville, 1977   JOHN KILLINGER

WEEK I

Only the person who has submitted to John's demand for repentance and cleansing can hope to meet the challenge of Jesus' way of living in the Kingdom. (Week I: Friday)

"Lord, I confess that I am like the crowds: I react much more excitedly to signs and wonders than I do to the mystery of forgiveness. Sharpen my perception more keenly to matters of the soul." (Week III: Saturday)

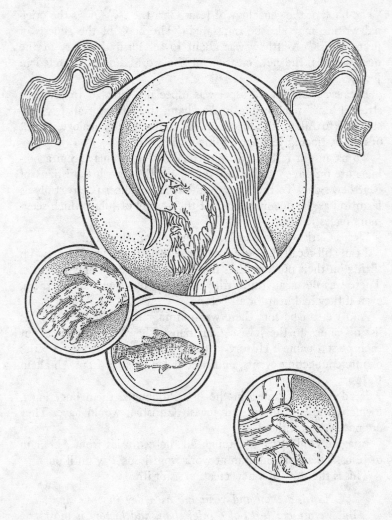

Week I: Sunday

"The book of the genealogy of Jesus Christ. . . ." Or, as the original writing may also be translated, "The book of the *genesis* of Jesus Christ." Matthew was about to set forth the story of the new Genesis, the new creation of the world, and it centered in Jesus.

Because Matthew's Gospel was especially directed to Jews, he stressed Jesus' relationship to Abraham, the father of all Jews, instead of to Adam, the first man. Therefore the genealogy, or list of names, tracing Jesus' royal line of descent.

To us, in our fast-paced impersonal society, it may seem a boring note on which to begin. Not so for the Jewish Christians of Matthew's day! To them it would have been sheer poetry, fully as beautiful as the opening verses of the Gospel of John, which seem more majestic to us.

"Jesus Christ, the son of David, the son of Abraham."

I can still recall the old folks in the little town where I grew up sitting on their porches after dark and discussing family histories. There was never anything trite or dull about such talk to them, even if they had heard it all before.

And we can be sure there was nothing trite or dull about this list of names to the Jewish Christians. They knew stories about each person named. History to them was a web, a ladder, a series of interconnecting events, and now it led directly from Abraham to Jesus.

Read over the names in the list. Pronounce them lingeringly, lovingly, the way an ancient Jewish Christian would have. They *are* poetry, aren't they?

Imagine God at work through all the centuries from Abraham to Jesus. Then imagine him at work from Jesus' day until ours.

This is the story of a new creation, isn't it?

> *O Lord, a thousand years are as a day in your sight.*
> *But we are creatures of a brief span, and history is most*

awesome to us. Teach us to honor our years by submit-
ting them to you. Let them be woven into the wonderful
pattern of your eternity. Let your new creation continue
in us. Through Jesus, who was descended from Abraham
and all these ancient people. Amen.

Week I: Monday

1:18–25 THE WORK OF GOD'S SPIRIT

The heavens and the earth, according to the first verses of the book of Genesis, were created by the Spirit of God. The Spirit moved over the face of the dark waters and brought forth the sun and the stars and the world.

Therefore Matthew, who was going to tell the story of the new creation in Jesus Christ, wished to emphasize the role of the Spirit in this new Genesis. His was a simple method, not at all unknown among the biographies of heroes in the ancient world: He spoke of a miraculous conception in which the Spirit actually fathered the child born to Mary.

The prophet Isaiah had promised long before that a virgin would conceive and bear a special child. His name would be called Emmanuel, or God with us.

God had been present in his first creation. The author of Genesis pictures him walking in the garden in the cool of the evening. Now, in the new creation, says Matthew, he is to be present in a different way. He is to be tempted, to suffer, and to die like one of us. It is a form of intimacy for which, as the Apostle Paul had already put it, the whole creation groaned until now. God will be in Christ, making the world his again.

Lord, it is exciting to think of your Spirit at work in
the world where I live, making the new creation out of
the old. I want to be part of the new creation. I want my
family and friends to be part of it. Help me to submit

5

my entire being to your Spirit, so that my life flows with
your purpose and not against it. Through Jesus, who has
shown us your Spirit. Amen.

Week I: Tuesday

2:1–12 WHAT MAKES MEN WISE?

Of all the miracles associated with the birth of Jesus, none seems more miraculous than the arrival of these strangers from the East. Apparently there were several of them. It has traditionally been assumed that there were three because three gifts are mentioned, but this is only an assumption.

Matthew's purpose in telling about them was to indicate the worldwide significance of the birth of the Christ. These travelers symbolized the eventual homage of all nations before the Son of God. They brought gifts usually associated with royalty. And for good reason—Jesus was destined to rule over all.

What could induce men like these to leave their homes and travel to distant lands? They said they had seen the star and knew that the prophecy concerning Jesus' birth in Bethlehem was about to be fulfilled.

That is amazing, when you think about it. The whole beings of these men appear to have been open to receive the messages of God in the universe around them. How different from the way most of us live! We are so preoccupied with matters of daily exist-ence that we rarely take time to watch and listen to the universe we live in. We develop spiritual myopia—an inability to see any-thing that doesn't concern our living or maintaining a household or enjoying a ballgame.

How many messages we miss—and how impoverished our lives are as a result.

> *Lord, I have eyes but I have learned to live without*
> *seeing. I am so insensitive. Teach me to have a sense of*

wonder again, the way I did as a child. Let me look at
everything as if for the first time, and marvel not at what
things are, but that they are. Through Jesus, who is the
greatest object of wonder. Amen.

Week I: Wednesday

2:13–18 CHRIST AND THE BEAST

Here is a part of the Christmas story we are prone to leave out—
the part about terror and cruelty and the provocation of evil. But
it ought to be there, every Christmas, for it is inseparable from
the birth of the holy child.

The book of Revelation ends with the struggle between Christ
and the Great Beast, the symbol of evil; and there is where the
gospel must really begin, as Matthew saw it. Herod, like most tyrants, felt extremely insecure. He probably did not believe that
God was ready to send a Messiah to Israel, but he did worry that
any popular figure might topple his precarious throne. So he
lashed out demonically at the news of Jesus' birth, and had all the
male children under two years of age in the town of Bethlehem
slain. Wails of agony must have gone up in many homes as
Herod's soldiers entered and dashed the babies against walls or
pulled them limb from limb.

What a tangled skein life is. The best that happens seems
somehow to call forth the worst too. Even the birth of the Savior
brought extra suffering into the lives of some.

How impossible it is to separate the wheat and the tares, the
good and the bad, in this life. As the Apostle Paul said, it is impossible even within a single life—the good we do, we have trouble doing, and the evil we would not do, we seem to do in spite of
ourselves. Can we hope that it will be any better with groups, institutions, and nations?

This is why, in many liturgical traditions, a prayer of confession
is set right at the heart of worship. Our only hope is in the right-

eousness of God, for we cannot claim any righteousness ourselves. We admit our mixed motives, impure thoughts, and failure to love our neighbors. It is the least we can do, for however much we belong to Christ, we are still troubled by the beast within.

> *O God, I long to be pure and honest and to deal thus with all persons. But I am too weak and unwise to fulfill the longing. Life is too complicated, and I often make wrong choices. Help me not to despair, but to rely more on you. Let me find in you the acceptance which enables me to live as well as I can with humility, courage, and compassion, accepting in others the weakness I find so deeply embedded in my own nature. Through Jesus, whose very presence often serves as the catalyst to clarify good and evil. Amen.*

Week I: Thursday

2:19–23 THE IMPORTANCE OF DREAMS

More dreams! First there was the one with the angel telling Joseph that God's Spirit was the father of the child she carried. Then there was the one warning him to take Mary and the child into Egypt. Now these additional dreams, in which he is advised to return to Israel and to settle in Galilee.

I wonder if we would follow advice we received in a dream.

Probably not. We belong to a culture which has put great emphasis on rationality. We have even developed rational explanations for dreams, so that we need not pay much attention to them. Many of us categorize dreams among hallucinations and disorders of the mind.

But some modern voices are saying that we do not pay enough attention to our dreams. And, if it is true that we reason better with our whole selves, not merely with our minds, then these messages may be of considerable importance.

Could it be that God uses our subconscious minds to implant

suggestions in us that our tougher conscious minds would reject? Perhaps our lives would be richer and more exciting if we only learned to trust our impulses from the unconscious more than we presently do.

When I have a hard decision to make, I pray as I fall asleep, "Speak to me in my dreams, O Lord," for I know I am more likely to hear there than in my busy waking hours.

> *Sometimes, Lord, you come to us in conscious modes. Other times you come when the mind is asleep and not watching. Help me to be so alive to the possibility of hearing your voice that I may hear in any way it comes to me. Through Jesus, who always heard.* Amen.

Week I: Friday

3:1—12 A FORERUNNER FOR THE TEACHER OF RIGHTEOUSNESS

Some scholars believe that John the Baptist was reared in or near the Essene community in Qumran, on the Dead Sea. The Essenes placed great emphasis on simple, righteous living and on ritual lustration or baptism.

Wherever John came from, his message and actions were an appropriate prelude to the ministry of Jesus, for what they called for most was a radical reordering of priorities, a total conversion of lifestyle. They became the background against which Matthew would shortly set the Sermon on the Mount, with its teachings of a transformed ethic for the new creation, and we cannot begin to understand those teachings if we forget this. Only the person who has submitted to John's demand for repentance and cleansing can hope to meet the challenge of Jesus' way of living in the Kingdom.

Already the word is laid down for the Pharisees and Sadducees, the people who think their religious affiliation will give them an advantage in entering the Kingdom. Tradition and heritage are only excess baggage in the day of the Lord. God can raise up new children for the Kingdom out of the very stones that crowd the riverbanks. (In Hebrew, there is a pun in this remark: *banîm* is children and *abanîm* is stones.) Christ's arrival will be a judgment on the falsely religious; they will be cut down like trees which do not bear fruit and burned like the useless chaff that is winnowed from the wheat.

> *Lord, help me to hear this stringent demand for personal conversion and righteousness, that I may soon be ready to consider the ethical teachings of Jesus when I read them. Let me depend on no artificial standards of worthiness as I come before you for judgment, but rely wholly on your grace to make me your child. Through Jesus, who baptizes the world with fire. Amen.*

Week I: Saturday

3:13–17 THE SIGN OF THE NEW CREATION

When the earth was created, God's Spirit hovered over the face of the waters. Now, in the new creation, the Spirit is identified with baptism, the ritual entry to the Kingdom.

This is why Jesus himself came to John to be baptized. John demurred because he stood in the presence of the one who was God's Spirit in the flesh. But Jesus insisted.

Human pride might have prevented our doing what Jesus did. We like to be begged, cajoled, and complimented into joining a movement.

But Jesus did not wait. He knew that a new age was coming into being. He came directly to the fiery prophet, to be baptized with all the others.

It was an important moment in human history, as was testified by the descent of the dove and the *bat qôl,* or voice out of heaven, saying, "This is my Son, my Beloved."

The full meaning of this strikes us only as we compare it with the story of Adam in the garden and God's disappointment in his failure to obey. Jesus' humility in accepting baptism "to fulfill all righteousness" was a sign of his willing obedience, and God was pleased. The new creation would not be hindered by the new Adam.

> *Lord, man baptizes with water and you baptize with the Holy Spirit. I need both, in order that your Kingdom may be fulfilled in me. Without the water, I hold myself apart from others in the Kingdom. Without the Spirit, the water is without effect. Fill me now with your Spirit, that I may be ready to meet the radical demands of the new age. Through Jesus, who has led the way as my Lord. Amen.*

WEEK II

Week II: Sunday

Matthew wrote his Gospel primarily as a catechism for teaching the Christian community what it needed to know. He must therefore have regarded prayer and fasting as very significant, to have placed this selection at the beginning of Jesus' public ministry.

We can only conclude that if prayer and fasting were so essential in Jesus' life, they must also be essential in ours today. But how many of us behave as if they were? We give them so little attention in our daily existence.

What if our lives were built around prayer and fasting?

First, we would live with a new awareness of the presence of God in all our affairs.

Second, the anxieties and fears which cripple us in the attempt to live full and meaningful lives would soon blow away like chaff from the wheat.

Third, we would perceive the world as gift instead of punishment. What had been wilderness to us would become a paradise where we had everything we truly needed.

We tend to associate prayer with miracles—with making things happen outside ourselves. But the greatest miracle prayer ever works is the transformation of the self so that it recognizes the blessings of God that lie around us all the time.

In other words, prayer reveals the Kingdom to us.

> *Lord, I have eyes to see but am often blind to the miracles around me. I have ears to hear but I usually talk so much that I cannot perceive what others are saying. Teach me quietness and wonder, O Lord, so that the glory of life can enter my senses and I can feel the abundance of your grace that is always present to me. Through Christ, who learned obedience through prayer and fasting. Amen.*

Week II: Monday

4:12–25 DOING GOD'S WILL IN GALILEE

Religion makes some of us headstrong. If God is with us, we think, then we ought to assume the most prominent positions as quickly as possible.

But here is our Lord doing exactly the opposite. Leaving Judea, the region around Jerusalem, he preached and taught in the remote area of Galilee. He even called two sets of brothers who were Galilean fishermen to become his most intimate followers. Together they traveled the countryside, interpreting the scriptures in synagogues as they went—in the country churches of their day!

Surely there is a lesson in this for us about working faithfully wherever God wants us to work. We are never required to serve in highly visible positions—only to apply ourselves cheerfully wherever we are.

Ironically, the greatest movements often begin in the least conspicuous places. The crowds which gathered around Jesus in Galilee soon spread his fame abroad, and people began coming from as far away as Jerusalem to hear his teachings and find healing for their infirmities.

> Lord, I suspect that Jesus' time of prayer and fasting in the desert prepared him for serving in inconspicuous places. I pray that my own seasons of devotion will leave me as filled with peace and contentment as he was, that I too may glorify you in humility and readiness to serve the poor. Amen.

Week II: Tuesday

5:1–12 A GREATER THAN MOSES

Matthew was writing his Gospel for people whose whole religious
life had once centered in the Torah, the Law brought down from
the mount by Moses. It was important therefore that they see
Jesus as the Moses of the new creation, the one whose teachings
from the mount would establish a Kingdom greater than the old
kingdom of Israel. Hence this "sermon," put together with edito-
rial license from sayings of Jesus which probably occurred in many
settings during his ministry.

It begins by defining who are the members of the new Kingdom
—the humble, the heavyhearted, the gentle, the righteous, the
merciful, the pure in heart, the peacemakers, the persecuted, the
maligned. At a stroke, Jesus sets these over against all the self-
righteous people who regarded themselves as the cream of the
godly society. We have but to recall the poor and outcast people
to whom he constantly ministered if we wish to see these descrip-
tions fleshed out. They were, after all, the little stones which John
the Baptist had said God could raise up into the true children of
Abraham.

The first Law, the Law of Moses, had been subject to misin-
terpretation. The Pharisees had followed it scrupulously, but had
missed the point of it. There would be no missing the point of
the new Law. Jesus made it plain that the Law was not to
supplant true devotion to God—even prostitutes and tax-collec-
tors could be numbered among the blessed ones. And finally, lest
even words like these in Matthew 5:1–12 be misconstrued, Jesus
died as one accursed under the Law of Moses. It was a new era!

> Lord, I need to remember what it is to be blessed,
> fortunate, happy. It is not necessarily to be well off. Nor
> are being in mourning, being persecuted, or being ma-
> ligned in themselves signs of well being. Instead, to be
> blessed is to be in Christ, to be in the Kingdom, regard-
> less of the state of my external affairs. It is to be yours

*in faithfulness despite whatever happens in the world.
Therefore I can mourn and say, "Yet how fortunate I
am," or I can be ill used and think, "There is still room
for happiness." Let the truth of this insight sustain me
through this day and the next. In the name of Jesus,
who died for what he taught. Amen.*

Week II: Wednesday

5:13–16 SALT AND LIGHT

"YOU are the salt of the earth. . . . YOU are the light of the
world." Read it with the right emphasis. Jesus was setting his disciples over against the old Israel, over against Judaism, over
against Mosaic religion. He wanted them to see that it was *they*,
not the priests and keepers of the old Law, for whom the world
was waiting. *They*, not the scribes and Pharisees, would be heralds
of the Kingdom. *They*, not the old rabbis, would bring spice and
light to the people of the earth.

Do we dare read ourselves into the "you"? Then the words
commit us to action. If we are salt, then we must season. If we are
light, then we must shine. For salt that does not season is thrown
out and light that does not shine is worthless.

Let your light shine, Jesus said, so that it gives illumination to
everyone and that those who see your good works will recognize
the glory of God in you.

This is no theology of good works Jesus was recommending, but
a theology of the glory of God. We bring seasoning and light to
the world, not that the world may praise us, but that it may see
and fall down before the presence of God in our midst. Salt is lost
in the flavoring of food; we do not praise the salt but the taste of
the food. Light is overlooked when it reveals the contents of a
room; we do not praise the light but the items on display.

So it is with us: The joy of our calling is to help people discover
the glory of God!

17

*Lord, being salt and light is a problem to me. I am
so inclined to seek people's attention for myself. I want
to have my flavor brought out and my qualities illumi-
nated. Help me to discover the richness of life when it
is dedicated to helping others to see you instead of me,
so that they praise your name instead of mine. Through
Jesus, who always reminded us that what he did was
through your presence and not his own power. Amen.*

Week II: Thursday

5:17–48 A MORE PERFECT WAY

Here is the Teacher of Righteousness at his most incisive!

Think of the battles of grace versus works that had already
swept through Christianity when Matthew wrote his Gospel. Paul
had had conflict after conflict with the Judaizers, the Jewish
Christians who insisted on the primacy of legalism in their newly
founded religion. The question was by no means settled.

How does Matthew resolve it? By grouping the teachings of
Jesus into a remarkable *both/and* combination.

No, you cannot work for the Kingdom, Jesus says—God *gives*
the Kingdom. He gives it to the humble, the mourners, the gentle, those who long for righteousness—all those who are described
in Matthew 5:3–12.

But of those to whom much is given much is expected. Now
that you are given the Kingdom, you must go beyond the dry
righteousness of the scribes and Pharisees, and fulfill the law in
love.

You have heard it said that you must not kill—you must not
even be angry with your brother.

You have heard it said that you must not commit adultery—
you must not even have lust in your heart for a person of the opposite sex.

The law says you may put away your wife by divorcing her—but that way you make a mere thing of her, and treat her as an adulteress, who has lain with you without love.

You have heard it said that you should not make false oaths—but you should not have to make any oaths at all, because your word should be your bond and you should do everything you say you will do.

You have heard that it is right to extract payment from everyone who owes you, even to the extent of an eye for an eye and a tooth for a tooth—but you should go all out for other persons, even those who are considered your enemies.

Jesus did not come to do away with the Law. The Law was never our problem. It was the human will that was the problem. When the will is bad, we can find ways of getting around any law or statute. Jesus came to tell us that God gives us the Kingdom without regard to the Law, but that, once we know that, we should desire to go far beyond the Law, obeying the highest impulses of the human soul. That way, and that way only, do we reveal the perfect way of God to the world.

That way only do we become the salt and light to the world.

> *Lord, I am an unworthy person. I have accepted the gift of your Kingdom without really considering what is an appropriate lifestyle for me as a child of the Kingdom. I am afraid I have obscured for others the true vision of life in the Kingdom. I have also robbed myself of the joy of total commitment to your way. Now that I see this, help me to catch the real spirit of the Kingdom. Let me not live with the law as a requirement to be met but as a guideline to go beyond. Through Jesus, whose understanding of these things sustained him even in the horror of crucifixion. Amen.*

Week II: Friday

6:1-23 A DEPTH OF HONEST PIETY

In the preceding passage, Jesus said that true righteousness lies not in fulfilling the demands of the Law but in going beyond them. Now he warns against mere superficial piety—practicing our religion in order to be seen by others.

When we give gifts to the poor, we are to do it quietly—so quietly, in fact, that one hand doesn't know what the other is doing.

When we pray, we are to do it without ostentation—even in a small room with the door shut. Nor are we to seek virtue through extremely long prayers, as though God sold his favor by the yard. We are to pray simply and economically, as the manifestation of a sincere and devoted spirit.

When we fast (remember that Jesus gave the model for fasting and praying in Matthew 4:1-11), we are not to screw our faces up and try to look like martyrs in our faith; on the contrary, we are to put on happy faces and not let on to others that we are fasting at all.

Doing these things to be seen by others is laying up treasures on earth, where they will not last. What we should be interested in is what God thinks about our piety. Our real treasure is with him.

As our bodies receive their vision from the eye, so our spiritual lives receive their light from the way we look at things. If we are shortsighted, and are concerned only about how other persons perceive our righteousness, then we shall be full of darkness. But if we see things truly, and realize that our religion is to be judged by God, not man, then we are living in the light.

> Lord, I am condemned by this brief prayer which Jesus told us to pray. To pray it, my whole life must be sincerely dedicated to you—must be in fact a prayer. When I pray, I am more wordy because I feel an awkwardness in our relationship—I have not been totally committed

to your will in my life. Forgive me, as I hope I am at peace with all persons, and let me glorify your name through honest religion in the days to come. Amen.

Week II: Saturday

6:24–34 SHALOM: THE TRUE PEACE OF GOD

Shalom, the Hebrew word for fullness and peace, was frequently heard among the Jews. But Jesus struck at the irony of a religion in which so many people spoke of *shalom* and so few people actually possessed it. Most Jews, he observed, were like the Gentiles—they clamored for food and clothing and security as if these were the most important things in their lives. True *shalom* had not become part of their lifestyle.

None of us, said Jesus, can worship both God and worldly possessions. If we care about mere things—if we pile them up in order to have plenty tomorrow—they inevitably interfere with our giving full attention to God.

How this cuts across the grain with us, just as it did in Matthew's day! We much prefer the theology occasionally found in the Old Testament which says that possessions are a sign of God's favor. But the New Testament seems to have a bias in favor of being poor—not because there is any special virtue in poverty itself, but because the poor are freer to respond to the radical demands of the Kingdom.

God's wayfarers in the world—that is how the New Testament pictures the disciples of Jesus. People like Peter and John, who, when accosted by the crippled beggar in Acts 3, had no silver or gold coins to give him but gave him instead the healing power that sprang from their dedication and purity of heart.

Peter and John had *shalom—really* had it—because they had left everything to follow Jesus. When will we learn there is no other way to have *shalom?*

Lord, I am really uncomfortable with one foot in the boat and one foot on the shore. I don't know why I try to live this way. It is an agony, really. I guess I am afraid to leave the land. But I see the inadequacy of this position, and ask for faith to commit myself entirely to the boat. Help me to launch out into the deep. Through Jesus, who will be in the boat with me. Amen.

WEEK III

Week III: Sunday

7:1–28 LIVE A SIMPLE LIFE AND LIVE IT WELL

Energy is the power of life, and each of us has only a certain amount of it, whether psychic or physical. We should be careful, then, how we spend it, and Matthew concludes the Sermon on the Mount by repeating some of Jesus' observations about living simply and living well.

We should not waste time and effort criticizing others. We have enough to do looking after our own failures.

We should not give ourselves to idle arguments or disputations with people who have no real interest in the Kingdom. Besides being pointless, it often works to our own detriment.

We should live in simple expectation that God will take care of us. Even an earthly father tries to meet the needs of his child. Can we not expect more of God?

We should do good to all other persons—even those outside the faith—just as we would like them to do good to us. This is, after all, the point of the Law and the prophets.

We should really concentrate on entering the Kingdom, because it is more demanding that many people realize. Few, in fact, really enter it; most simply follow the crowds, thinking they are entering.

We should cling to sound teaching and avoid self-appointed prophets and teachers who are only taking advantage of some people's confusion. You can usually tell who these false leaders are by measuring them against the teachings in this sermon. Unfortunately, they lead many people astray, and these people are going to be disappointed in the end and protest that they were great servants of the Lord; but the Lord will tell them they were mistaken.

The way to be sure you are moving in the right direction is to live by the words of this sermon. It is like a rock you can build your house on. Then, when the time of the winds and rains comes, and other people's efforts are being swept along in the swirling waters, yours will stand fast.

Lord, I know why people thought Jesus had real authority, and did not speak empty things he had borrowed from other people. It was because his life was real and because he spoke to the depths in their own hearts. I know he speaks to the deep places in mine. He makes all other philosophies seem so cheap and selfish in comparison. I want the Kingdom to be a reality in my life, Lord. I don't want to be like those poor people who spent their lives on the wrong things. Help me to build well on these teachings without turning them into a new legalism. Through Jesus, whose gift to us on the cross is the surest guarantee of the validity of everything he taught. Amen.

Week III: Monday

8:1-4 THE POWER TO HEAL

After the section on Jesus' teachings, Matthew now turns to reports of his healing power. The very first story, of the healing of a leper, continues the theme we touched on earlier, that Jesus is greater than Moses, who gave the Torah.

The Torah, in Leviticus 13 and 14, gave very specific instructions about persons having leprosy. At the very first sign of an itching sore, they were to present themselves to the priest. If he verified that they had contracted leprosy, then they must go outside the community and live alone until they either died or were cured of the dread disease. In the event of a miraculous cure, the healed person was to present himself to the priest, who would determine whether the person was indeed relieved of the disease. If the priest decided that the person was cured, he would kill a bird, dip a living bird in its blood, sprinkle some blood on the cured person, and release the living bird to fly away as he pronounced the person well.

Moses' memory was sacred among the Jews because he was the

giver of the Law. But here was one who could do more than give a law about a person with leprosy—he could heal the person! Jesus reached out and touched a man, says Matthew, and immediately the man was cleansed of his disease.

Finally, as if to emphasize again that he had come to fulfill the Law, not to destroy it, Jesus told the man to go to the priest and make an offering of the two birds as Moses had commanded.

> *I am awed, O Lord, by the power of this man Jesus, who could touch a leprous man and make him whole again. I am also awed by his self-control in telling the man to go and show himself to the priest and fulfill the Torah. He must really have been in touch with himself to do that—and in touch with you. Help me to enter into this mystery too. In the name of the Healer.* Amen.

Week III: Tuesday

8: 5–17 MORE HEALINGS

Two more, to be precise. The servant of the Roman centurion, and Peter's mother-in-law. And then all those nameless ones who were brought with demons and illnesses.

Why did Matthew choose these two stories out of the hundreds he might have known?

The centurion probably represented the non-Jewish world, much as the narrative of the magi had symbolized it in the birth episode. Even though his Gospel was intended primarily for Jewish Christians, because he was at such pains to point out how Jesus fulfilled the Old Testament prophecies, Matthew obviously wanted to say something here to include all the non-Jews who had become Christians.

"Many will come from east and west," said Jesus, "and sit at table with Abraham, Isaac, and Jacob in the kingdom of heaven, while the sons of the kingdom will be thrown into the outer darkness."

As for Peter's mother-in-law—well, Peter had become something very special in the history of the church, and this little domestic touch would have meant much to the early Christians. The story is not entirely unlike the other. After all, Peter was an outsider to the Pharisees too—one of the little folk, the people of the land, who were practically illiterate on important religious questions. And a mother-in-law would have enjoyed almost as little status as a servant. She was, in effect, a nobody. But even the nobodies are included in the gifts brought by Jesus.

> *Lord, nobody could be more of an outsider to the faith of Israel than I. I'm not of the first century, I don't speak the language, I don't know the traditions. Yet you have opened your Kingdom to me. Why, Lord? It is a wonder too deep to contemplate. I can only marvel and live in constant thankfulness. In the name of the one who extended power to nobodies.* Amen.

Week III: Wednesday

8:18–22 SAYINGS FOR DISCIPLES

These two sayings, involving would-be disciples, are interesting for their emphasis on the radical demands which Jesus laid upon those who would follow him.

First, the scribe who was awed at Jesus' teachings and vowed to follow him wherever he went. He did not know what he was saying, apparently, and Jesus apprised him: "Foxes have holes, and birds of the air have nests; but the Son of man has nowhere to lay his head." Two suggestions leap from this saying—one, of the restless, itinerant nature of Jesus' ministry, and the other, of the stature of the man. "Son of man," *huios tou anthrōpou*, is one of several messianic titles found in the scriptures. Albright and Mann, in the Anchor Bible translation, render this title "The Man," insisting that it means "Representative Man" as in the book of Daniel. Either way, Jesus identifies himself with the end-time of history and as a cosmic figure who should lack a specific residence. The person who wished to follow him was thus reminded that it was no little movement he would attach himself to, and that it was not one from which he could turn back at any time he desired.

Second was the follower who wished to come with Jesus after a brief delay for burying his father (Jewish law required burial within twenty-four hours). "Follow me," said Jesus, "and leave the dead to bury their own dead." What is the meaning of this apparently harsh answer? Would a day have made that much difference? Perhaps Jesus was underlining the demand for obedience in those who became his disciples. Or perhaps he was emphasizing the difference between the old era, the era of the Torah, and the new, the era of the Messiah, in which case he was saying in effect, "When you follow me, you are entering a completely new age; let those who belong to the old age take care of their own." Whatever the meaning, it is clear that the emphasis was on total commitment to the Messiah.

> *Lord, I have trouble with the tone of these verses. There is a streak of stubborn independence in me that doesn't want to surrender to you. Is the character of the new age such that I must surrender in order to be a disciple? It really bothers me, Lord. Help me to deal with the distress this causes me, and to do it in such a way that I become a more faithful servant. Through Jesus, who both assures and frightens me. Amen.*

Week III: Thursday

8: 23–27 THE LORD OF THE WINDS AND SEA

Matthew now narrates three separate incidents depicting the extraordinary power of Jesus—the calming of the sea (8:23–27), the casting out of demons from two Gadarene demoniacs (8:28–34), and the forgiving and healing of a paralytic (9:1–8).

One of the remarkable things about the narrative of the storm, when we think about it, is that the cry for help came from disciples, some of whom were fishermen, men of the sea. For years the sea had been their second home. They had surely ridden out many a storm, for storms were likely to arise quickly on the Sea of Galilee. Why this sudden evidence of fear and distrust in their own ability to survive? We can only surmise that the storm's fury was greater than any they had seen before, and that in the height of the churning clouds and the depth of the troughs opening in the water they were genuinely afraid they would perish.

Jesus was the center of *shalom* through all of this. The violence of the storm did not even awaken him. The men had to shake him and cry out to him that they were on the verge of dying. Turning his face toward them (Mark records that he had been sleeping on a pillow), he asked why they had so little faith. Then he stood and transferred the calm that was in him to the sea itself, and to the winds, so that everything became still.

"What sort of man is this," marveled the experienced seamen, "that even winds and sea obey him?"

> *Lord, does this story suggest that you are more the master of my situation—my home, my context, my business—than I am, just as you were master of the fishermen's sea? If it does, then maybe I had better rethink the matter of who is in charge here.* Amen.

Week III: Friday

8:28–34 LORD OVER DEMONS

"What have you to do with us, O Son of God?" cried the demons. "Have you come here to torment us before the time?" Matthew surely used this story to emphasize that Jesus was recognized as the Messiah even by the spirits that inhabit people. In

Enoch, a Jewish apocalypse, demons are said to have power until the day of judgment. Here, in Matthew, they realize that Jesus is the bringer of that day of judgment, though the final catastrophic day has not arrived.

The passage also indicates again the universal character of Jesus' messiahship, for he is in Gentile country, not Jewish (hence the herd of pigs), and these particular demons inhabit two men who are not Jewish.

In Mark's Gospel (5:1–20) there is only one demoniac, and, when Jesus has used his power to exorcise the demons, the man becomes the focus of attention for the townspeople who come out to see the effects of the miracle. But Matthew, who has possibly combined the Marcan account with another in Mark 1:23–28, so that there are two possessed men instead of one, has the crowds come out to see Jesus, not the cured demoniacs. It is a subtle change, perhaps, but an important one: It is who the Messiah is that is important in all of these stories, not what is done in the stories. He is the Lord of the new creation, and that is the theme that matters to Matthew.

Mark makes it plain why the men begged him to leave their part of the country: they were afraid. Unaccustomed to witnessing such displays of power, they asked Jesus to go away. They preferred to keep matters the way they were.

> Lord, I would probably have been right in there with those townspeople, if I had been there, asking you to move on to some other territory. It is the dullness in me. I prefer an almost intolerable status quo, which I know, to any kind of interference-with-that-status-quo which I don't know. Help me to get beyond that, Lord, and be ready for any new thing you introduce into my life. Cast out the demon of my dullness, and let me follow you. Amen.

Week III: Saturday

9: 1–8 THE AUTHORITY TO FORGIVE AND THE
POWER TO HEAL

This story goes beyond the preceding miracle stories in Matthew because it raises the question of Jesus' authority to forgive sins. Mark's account of the same story (2:1–12) makes the problem more explicit: Only God can forgive sins. Jesus was accused of blasphemy, therefore, because he was exercising the divine right to forgive.

This would have been a ticklish issue with the Jews, for whom the matter of forgiveness was institutionalized into a system of priests and sacrifices. Jesus was flying in the face of the entire system by telling the paralytic that he was forgiven. But Matthew apparently set the story here for two reasons: to indicate the growing conflict between Jesus and the scribes (and by implication the Pharisees), and to further enhance the picture he has already drawn of Jesus as the leader greater than Moses, who was able to deliver the Law but unable to exercise the priestly function of absolving guilt.

The healing miracle, which to human flesh would seem to require more power than forgiving sin, was performed in the story as a sign of authority which the people could understand. And, while we do not know the reaction of the scribes to this, the crowds, as is often the case in Matthew's Gospel, respond as though electrified, glorifying God for having sent such authority among them in the flesh.

> Lord, I confess that I am like the crowds in this story:
> I react much more excitedly to signs and wonders than
> I do to the mystery of forgiveness, which is much less
> visible. Sharpen my perception that I may look more
> keenly to these matters of the soul which are often more
> important than the merely physical functions of the body.
> Through Jesus, who saw at once that this paralytic needed
> forgiveness more than he needed locomotion. Amen.

31

WEEK IV

"Tell John what you see—the blind recover sight, the deaf hear, the lame walk, the dead and dying are raised up." (Week IV: Thursday)

"Lord, teach me to care so much for everyone affected by my power that I may not abuse it, but may turn it into a blessing shared with others." (Week VI: Sunday)

Week IV: Sunday

9:9–13 A KINGDOM OF SINNERS

Most scholars do not believe that the Matthew mentioned here was actually the author of this Gospel, but the story is told with the probable intention of linking the name of the disciple to the Gospel.

Tax collectors were held in disdain by religious Jews not so much because they worked for the occupying power as because they handled money with pagan inscriptions and drawings on it. The sinners referred to, moreover, were probably nonobservant Jews, not grossly disreputable people. Both the tax collectors and the sinners were apparently friends of Matthew who gathered in his home with Jesus and the other disciples after Matthew decided to give up his office to be a follower of Jesus.

The Pharisees, who were among the thirty or forty persons who probably stood around the room in Matthew's home, mumbled to the disciples their amazement that this famous rabbi was eating with nonobservant persons. Jesus, as happens several times in the Gospel, overhears remarks not intended for him and answers them. He cites Hosea 6:6—"I desire mercy, and not sacrifice"— and says he came to call sinners, or nonobservers, not the traditionally righteous people.

We must remember that Judaism was very strong toward the end of the century when this Gospel was written, despite the overthrow of Jerusalem in A.D. 70, and that there was much wrangling between the Christians and the Judaizers. This narrative would have been a strong document in struggles such as that between Paul and the Judaizers in the Galatian churches.

Again, as promised by John the Baptist, it is a case of God's raising up new children of Abraham from the stones along the river of baptism.

Lord, I have the same problem as the Pharisees: I tend to expect you in the old familiar places, behaving in traditional ways. Therefore I do not watch for you to

36

break out in new places, doing new things. Forgive this
shortsightedness in me, and help me to be more open. I
do not want to miss the evidences of your presence in
my own day and my own society. Through Jesus, whose
freshness and authority seem always to have lain in his
power to see clearly. Amen.

Week IV: Monday

9:14–17 THE PRESENCE OF THE BRIDEGROOM

This passage is easily linked to the preceding one because it has to
do with nonobservance. John the Baptist's disciples ask Jesus why
it is that they fast as the Pharisees do, while the disciples of Jesus
do not. The specific references of the passage may have been intended by the author as a rejection by Jesus of identification with
the Essenes or other practitioners of cultic righteousness.

The ground for the rejection would be the fact that Jesus is
someone special. He is the bridegroom and center of a celebration. He is the one greater than Moses. He is the Messiah, the
Lord of the new creation.

There is apparently a reference to the death of the Messiah—
the bridegroom will be taken away from the wedding guests—and
then the guests shall fast again as others do. But for the moment
they are enjoying a foretaste of the great eschatological wedding,
the end of all things in God's new era.

In that final time, Jesus seems to indicate, the Torah or Law of
Moses will be left behind. To try to graft the Kingdom onto it
would be like putting a new, unshrunken patch on an old garment
that has been washed many times, or like putting powerful new
wine into old skins that no longer have the flexibility to endure
much expansion. Therefore observances such as calendrical fasting
(as opposed to fasting for self-discipline) are matters of mere fuss-
iness among the followers of Jesus, and hardly worth attention.

As Jesus said to the Pharisees in Matthew's house, God desires mercy, not sacrifice—which is far more demanding than the old system of laws and regulations.

> *Lord, there is something comfortable about a rule or a law. It helps us to know where we stand. And there is something frightening about Jesus' way of saying we are beyond that now and are ruled by a spirit, not a regulation. It sort of takes my breath. I hope I am ready for this. Give me the faith to live in the new era. Through Jesus, the bridegroom. Amen.*

Week IV: Tuesday

9:18–38 JESUS AND THE CROWDS

Here Matthew gives us an impressionistic picture of the busy ministry of Jesus. Everywhere he turned there were people to be helped, people from all levels of society, including even the president of the local synagogue. And each time Jesus performed a miracle of healing or resuscitation, his reputation grew that much more, so that ever greater crowds pressed at his elbow.

"Nothing like this has ever been seen in Israel," proclaimed the people. Not even Moses or Elijah had been able to do such things. Jesus was clearly the one appointed to usher in the new creation.

Traveling from town to town announcing the new era and curing the people, Jesus felt deeply for the persons who had such need. They were like poor bleating sheep, stumbling over one another in every direction because they had no leaders.

The old Mosaic order had run its course and was doing the masses little good. It was time for a new leader, time for a new order, a new creation. But the new creation would not come in of its own; it required many colaborers, the way a ripe crop requires many persons for immediate harvesting.

Pray for such workers, said Jesus. Beg the owner of the crop to send them in where the need is so great. It is time for a new thing to be done in Israel.

I see an image, Lord, of thousands of people entering an enormous field where the corn fairly bursts to be picked. They are a motley crew—literate and illiterate, rich and poor, gifted and clumsy. And they all enter for one reason—to harvest the heavy crop. I pray for them, Lord—the missionaries and ministers and teachers and nonprofessional Christians alike—and offer myself to be one of them. Through Jesus, who looked on crowds with great compassion. Amen.

Week IV: Wednesday

10: 1–42 INSTRUCTIONS FOR DISCIPLES

Imagine yourself in Jesus' place. You have called twelve disciples and they have been with you for months now, learning about the Kingdom and helping with the crowds of people as you taught them and healed the sick. Now you are ready to send them out singly or in small groups all over the country. What would you say to them on the eve of their departure?

Here are Jesus' instructions to them. They are very practical, and in keeping with what he has told them about life in the Kingdom.

The disciples' major responsibility is to proclaim the arrival of the Kingdom, heal the sick, cleanse the lepers, cast out demons, and raise the dead or dying.

They are to take no money for any of this, except such as is necessary to live from place to place. (Already by the time Matthew wrote this, some persons had tried to use the gifts of the Spirit for personal gain. See the account of Simon Magus in Acts 8:4–24.)

They are to behave properly, and, if any household or town fails to receive them, simply shake the dust from their feet as they leave—what one writer has called "the sacrament of failure," to be performed over the hard cases that must be left behind.

They should expect difficulties—prison, quarreling, divided households, death. (By the time of this Gospel's writing, the disciples had probably encountered all these obstacles in abundance.) Yet they are not to fear, for they do the work of God and he is with them. He who considers every sparrow of the field will not fail to note their every peril.

Not the least of the disciples' difficulties will be from their own families. Parents will not want sons and daughters to go as workers in this seemingly impossible undertaking, nor will children wish their parents to go. But a life given for the Kingdom, whatever the immediate cost, is a life fulfilled.

It is an exciting venture the disciples set out upon, for they go in the name of Jesus and anyone who receives them is actually receiving him. Even a cup of cold water handed to one of them along the way will have its reward.

> Lord, it must have been terribly demanding to be one of the first disciples. There weren't any churches for them to preach in, or any Christian communities to offer them support. They were obviously committed people. I pray for today's ministers, Lord, that they may know similar commitment. Remind them that the power and the Kingdom are yours, and that all that is required of them is to be faithful to the vision. Through Jesus, who still calls and sends out disciples. Amen.

Week IV: Thursday

11:1–19 JESUS AND JOHN THE BAPTIST

It was natural for John to raise the question, wasn't it? He was alone and in prison, probably treated like an animal, miles from the countryside and riverbanks he loved. A man can become desperately uncertain about things in a situation like that.

"Tell John," Jesus said, "what you see—the blind recover sight, the deaf hear, the lame walk, the dead and dying are raised up."

It was a definitive answer. What more was there to say? The Kingdom and its Lord were obviously there.

Afterwards, Jesus mused on the rough old prophet. Surely no mother's son on earth was greater than John. Yet, said Jesus, in the Kingdom every one is as great as John—the Kingdom is an equalizer.

The times were violent, the way the weather is when a cold front and a warm front collide, and John, tough as he was, had gotten caught in the violence. Jesus himself would be crucified, but he was up to it. Is it possible that he was even a rough and violent man, as John was? The satire in his language in verses 7–10 may indicate that he was.

People are funny, Jesus was thinking. John came as an abstemious religious figure, eating little and refusing strong drink, and people said he was crazy. Jesus came as the opposite, eating and drinking with nonobservant Jews, and the very same people said he was a glutton and a drunkard. Yet God's purpose was being worked out in both of them.

It is amazing, isn't it, how many ways God works?

> *Lord, this is such a human passage. I can almost hear Jesus laughing with joy as he told those men to go tell John what they saw. He had such utter confidence in it all. And that reverie about John—he really cared for John, the way a man cares for another man who has done a good job. And that reflection on people too—Jesus was no fool, Lord. He knew the price of things, didn't he? I can follow more joyfully for this passage, Lord. Thanks.*

Week IV: Friday

11:20–30 GOD AND THE SIMPLE FOLK

Ah, the disappointment breaks through here for the towns that had already proven inhospitable to the Kingdom's work. Even Capernaum, which had been Jesus' headquarters, had rejected the new creation. They had all written their own judgments, but the chief strategist of the new age was disappointed.

There is a touch of sadness and irony in his thanksgiving. God has indeed begun his new creation in the simple folk—the untutored people of the land, who don't stand very high in anybody's social register. They have rallied to the Kingdom.

Let them flock to him—the hard-working poor, the little people of the land—and he will give them relief. Let them join him in the yoke—they will find him gentle and humble-hearted like themselves. Together, they will bring in the Kingdom.

The sophisticated townspeople and the religious leaders are too preoccupied with other things to care about the Kingdom; but God will build it yet from the little stones along the riverbank!

> Lord, I always liked countryfolk. They don't take things for granted the way city people do. They are affected by the rain, the smell of the earth, the movement of birds. There is an openness and honesty about them, bred by the land they work on. They are more in touch with themselves than city dwellers. And they are still working for the Kingdom. God bless the peasants and the farmers. Through Jesus, who found them receptive. Amen.

Week IV: Saturday

12:1–14 LORD OF THE SABBATH

As is often the case in Matthew's Gospel, the spirit and thrust of the new creation are here set over against those of the old. Under the Torah, which was the chief religious expression of the old order, some people had fallen into a way of life characterized by mere legal nitpicking; among the thirty-nine varieties of work which their excessive legalism forbade was the plucking of grain on the Sabbath. But the spirit of Jesus' Kingdom shatters this narrow philosophy the way new wine shatters old wineskins.

First Jesus reminds the Pharisees that David himself had once set a precedent for eating food forbidden by religious scruples when the scruples are transcended by the fact of simple hunger. Then he cites an additional biblical reference, Numbers 28:9–10, and throws the discussion into another key altogether: The priests in the temple profane the Sabbath by performing their duties on the holy day, and are guiltless in doing so; and, as he himself is Lord of the new creation, his disciples are as free to do whatever he permits them as the priests of the old order!

There is a different accent here than in Mark's account of the same event (Mark 2:23–28). In Mark, Jesus says, "The sabbath was made for man, not man for the sabbath; so the Son of man is Lord even of the sabbath" (verses 27–28). In other words, man himself takes precedence over mere legalism. But Matthew omits the humanistic reference, repeats his earlier usage of Hosea 6:6 ("I desire mercy, and not sacrifice"), and interprets this verse as a repudiation of the old order in favor of the new. That is, God took no pleasure in the excessive legalism of the old system; he has given his creation over to the Son of man, the Messiah, who is Lord of the Sabbath as he is Lord of everything else. The Pharisees are guilty not only of offending humanity, but of accusing the Lord himself.

Proceeding to the synagogue, where there is a man with a withered hand, Jesus is taunted by some persons there over whether it is permissible to heal on the Sabbath. With the same *élan* he has shown in the earlier episode, Jesus reminds them that their laws permit them to rescue animals on the Sabbath, and asks if a man isn't of more value than an animal. Ignoring the likely rejoinder that rescuing animals is considered an emergency but that there is no reason a static condition such as a lame hand cannot wait until the following day, Jesus tells the man to put forth his hand and heals it.

It is no wonder the Pharisees go away angrily and seek ways to destroy Jesus. His whole tone and temper are different from theirs. His disregard for legalism is only a handy excuse; the fact is, they cannot bear the new order which he represents.

> *Lord, how clearly Jesus saw what the true priorities in life are, and how easily we confuse them. We are always setting into motion systems which run away from us and begin to oppress people—in government, in education, in business, in human relations. Help us to see when this happens and be willing to terminate or modify them as much as is necessary for the good of those affected by them. Through the one whose courage led to a cross. Amen.*

WEEK V

Week V: Sunday

12:15–21 THE SECRET OF JESUS

When the time comes that you are well known to all men, said the poet Rainer Maria Rilke, then it is time to take another name —any name—so that God can call you in the night.

Here, in fulfillment of a prophecy in Isaiah, Matthew indicates the becoming modesty of Jesus as his fame grew throughout Israel. To be sure, there was an external reason for his asking those he healed not to tell anyone—the opposition of the Pharisees was growing and he did not wish to provoke a final encounter before his hour had come (cf. John 12:27, 13:1). But the quiet manner which Isaiah predicted for the Messiah accords well with the injunctions in Matthew 6 against making any display of piety or good works. Jesus was not letting his left hand know what the right hand had done.

People appreciate modesty. The greatest persons in the world are usually the most self-effacing. Their strong sense of inner worth renders unnecessary the praise of the multitudes. It is the diminutive persons, the would-be heroes, who make a show of their gifts and achievements.

Lord, why is it that those of us who do least for others are most concerned to be recognized for what we have done? We desire thank-you notes, brass plaques, and public praise for all our good deeds. Help us to be more like the Master of men, who, having rendered the greatest of services, besought others to remain silent about the gift. Amen.

Week V: Monday

12:22–37 JESUS SPEAKS BACK

Jesus may have been a gentle and modest person, but he was also firm with those who opposed him. In this passage there are echoes of John the Baptist, whose fiery denunciation of the scribes and Pharisees once rang out along the Jordan.

The Pharisees had said that Jesus derived his power from the Evil One. How, he demanded to know, could the Evil One bring forth good works? Obviously it was the Pharisees themselves who were related to the Evil One. They were a nest of snakes, hissing and writhing and ready to inject their poison into any victim who came near them!

It was not that Jesus minded their words against him—those would be forgiven. But their impediment to the movement of the Spirit of God, to the coming of the Kingdom, was unforgivable. In the day of judgment, their own words would prove their condemnation.

Here is a healthy attitude for all of us! We should not worry about what others say or think of us, but we should always be concerned about the spirit of evil which blocks the Kingdom's work in the world. *That* is the real problem we face.

> Lord, I often get steamed up over the wrong things— little slights from friends or a lack of recognition from those I work for—while I hardly think of the graft and corruption at the corporate level which are grinding down your little ones, making slums of our cities, and poisoning the atmosphere of our world. Help me to become more passionate about the important things. Through Jesus, who had the right perspective. Amen.

Week V: Tuesday

12:38–50 SIMPLE FOLK REQUIRE NO PROOF

How easy it is to think, "If only I had lived in Jesus' day and seen the miracles he worked, I would have had no problem believing in him!" But Jesus said to the scribes and Pharisees that only a perverse generation needs a sign in order to believe, and he refused to accommodate their desire for a sign—except to speak of his own death and resurrection, which Matthew obviously regards as the most important sign he ever gave. They would fare worse in the judgment than the people of ancient Nineveh or the Queen of the South—non-Jews who respected God more than they did!

The scribes and Pharisees had tried, in their vain efforts to be righteous, to cleanse their lives of evil. But the evil had returned to its source seven times stronger than when it began. What hope could there be for such stiff-necked people?

By contrast, there were the disciples, who had never thought of themselves as righteous or skilled in the Law. They were like brothers and sisters and parents to Jesus. They had followed him without asking for signs of his power and authority. They were like the gentle, humble people of the Beatitudes. Theirs would be the Kingdom of God.

> Forgive me, Lord, for having ever desired signs of your favor. I am surrounded by such signs if I will only learn to see them. Life bears abundant clues of your presence, from the gentle sunlight that awakened me this morning to the water I drank from an old dipper to the lovely yellow squash on my plate at dinner and the smiles of my family around the table. Why am I so obtuse that I seldom recognize you? Thank you for being there, and for Jesus, who made such things much plainer to us. Amen.

Week V: Wednesday

13:1–23 SPEAKING IN PARABLES

Matthew 13 is given solely to parables about the Kingdom and discourse about parables. It is both tantalizing in its material and enlightening about Jesus' method of teaching. Contrary to the image we received from Matthew 5:1, of Jesus addressing the multitudes with the Sermon on the Mount, Matthew 13:34–35 asserts that Jesus "never spoke to them without a parable." This may mean that Jesus left the crowds to go up to the mountain and teach the disciples, and that the rich body of ethical teachings in Matthew 5–7 was really delivered to the inner circle of followers, not to the masses.

Why would Jesus have spoken to the crowds only in parables? Perhaps it was so the ones God intended to hear and be saved would recognize the true meaning of the parables, while others would hear only puzzling words and would not be affected by them. In this sense, a parable has been called "a trap for meaning." Its relevance is apparent only as one enters the story and acts out the drama. If the person hearing is successful, then the story becomes his or her story—it is no longer an impersonal narrative. Otherwise the story remains a mere absurdity.

We can only conclude that the explanation of the parable of the seeds in verses 18–23 and the later explanation of the parable of the wheat and tares in verses 36–43 are additives or glosses on the original text for the purpose of instructing neophyte Christians in the day when the Gospel was written. Jesus clearly expected the original disciples to understand the parables without explanation; if they did not, then there was no reason for him to speak in parables at all.

> Lord, the disciples heard and understood because their lives were committed to you. But I am often like the crowds who heard but never understood. At least, like them, I am seldom swept away from my usual moorings to enter the unchartered seas of the Spirit. The very monotony of my existence accuses me of never having heard

49

and responded fully to you. My meager response has been like that of the ground where the thistles lay—my own cares have grown faster than my concern for the Kingdom and have choked it out. I long for matters to be different, Lord. Increase my power to hear these parables as I read them again. Let me truly live them, from the inside out. Through Jesus, who tempts me with such mysteries. Amen.

Week V: Thursday

13:24–43 THE SECRET GROWTH OF THE KINGDOM

The one element common to all three of these parables is the way the Kingdom grows quietly, unobtrusively, and then one day becomes suddenly apparent to all.

The wheat grows silently among the tares until the time of harvest. Then the tares are cut down and destroyed, while the wheat is harvested and garnered into barns.

The lowly mustard seed, smaller than the seed of a cantaloupe or squash, grows quietly into a stalky plant towering over the plants from other small seed, and the birds come to light in it and survey the other plants below.

A tiny amount of leaven or yeast is mixed with a much larger amount of flour. It is invisible to the eye when they have been combined. Yet in a few hours it has quietly spread throughout the dough and caused it to expand to double and triple its original size.

It is always easier, isn't it, to see the evil at work in the world. Our daily papers and newscasts focus on the horrors and atrocities of the world around us. But the good news of the Kingdom is that it is growing too, though quietly and without notice, and that those who have ears to hear may realize this and exult in hope.

When I am appalled at the intensity of violence and rage in the modern world, Lord, help me to remember that the Kingdom has been growing quietly and steadily for centuries now, and that it is stronger and more widespread than anyone knows. Remind me of the unexpected people and places where I have had glimpses of its existence, and let me figure from that the almost limitless possibilities for its success in the world. Through Jesus, who could speak thus confidently despite the impending horror of the cross and the defection of his friends. Amen.

Week V: Friday

13:44–52 MORE PARABLES

"For sheer joy," says the New English Bible, the man who found the buried treasure "went and sold everything he had, and bought that field."

We can picture the man racing about from acquaintance to acquaintance, asking whatever they would give him for his possessions.

"But you don't want to sell those candlesticks, Barnabas—they belonged to your uncle Joseph."

"I want to sell—give me anything!"

"But Barnabas—your library! You have always loved it so!"

"No matter—it is nothing. What will you give?"

Joyously, confidently, vigorously selling *all* for the field with its treasure. So it is, said Jesus, with the Kingdom. If a man only knew its worth, he would give up everything for it.

This was the difference between Jesus and the scribes and Pharisees—he was enthusiastic, filled with the Spirit of the Kingdom. His mind raced from image to image, describing the coming of a new creation.

Even a teacher of the Law, he said, can become a learner in the Kingdom. Then he will not merely draw on the store of what has been written and said before, but will feel the tides of creation rise within him, so that he speaks new things as well as old.

How beyond price the Kingdom is—if men would only realize it!

> *The old and the new, Lord. How wonderful if all people were so open to both the past and the future, and could draw upon one while learning of the other. Grant that I may maintain a spirit which combines both reverence for what has been thought and taught in the past and receptivity for all the emergent factors which make for a new order in my time. Through Jesus, who said we could learn from him. Amen.*

Week V: Saturday

13:53–58 DISDAINING THE FAMILIAR

I went to school with one of the most famous theologians of modern times. We were not friends, but I used to see him frequently in the library, the halls, and the room where we ate our lunches. Like others who knew him even marginally during those days, I have great difficulty believing that he is the same man whose name is spoken with respect throughout the world. He was simply too common and unattractive to have evolved into that other person. In order to read his writings with proper reverence, I have to detach myself from any memory of the student I saw, and think of him only as a renowned theologian.

Apparently it was this way for the people of Jesus' hometown. They could not believe that the profound teachings they heard from Jesus or the miraculous healings he performed came from one whom they had watched growing up as the son of Mary. And the attention which they paid to the contrast between their expectancies and the man who stood before them diverted them from the things he was trying to say and do, so that his effectiveness was limited in their midst.

What they needed to remember, as we do, is that wisdom is a gift of God, whatever the vehicle, and we should not permit our incredulity toward the source to blind us to its value.

> *Lord, sometimes my children stagger me with their insights into life's mysteries. Help me never to miss the truth of what they say because I am so preoccupied with its source. The same goes for all the other places where I seldom expect to find wisdom. Through Jesus, who both said and did the truth. Amen.*

WEEK VI

Week VI: Sunday

14:1-12 THE DEATH OF THE BAPTIST

God is not the only judge of men. History—the long look—also renders its judgment. And history reveals the vast difference between the two men at the center of this little drama.

John we know to have been a simple man of simple tastes. Herod's life was complicated by ambition, pride, and foolishness.

John was morally zealous. Herod was corrupt and entangled in his own sins. He had broken Jewish law to divorce his wife and marry Herodias, and he broke it by executing John without a trial and by executing him by decapitation.

John was totally committed to the coming Kingdom of God. Herod was committed to keeping his own throne intact if he could.

John died with honor, and is remembered throughout the world as the forerunner of Christ. Herod died in disgrace, banished by the emperor to the remoter districts of Gaul, cut off from the very kingdom he sought so desperately to preserve.

Real security, history seems to say, does not lie in earthly thrones and fortifications, but in commitment to God and his righteousness. It cannot be bought by gold and jewels. It is given to those who live in the Spirit of God.

> Lord, power in the hands of a careless person is a frightening thing. It even prompts me to consider whether I do not often misuse the modest power at my disposal. Teach me to care so much for everyone affected by my power that I may not abuse it, but may turn it into a blessing shared with others. Through Jesus, who cared about the use of power. Amen.

Week VI: Monday

14:13–21 FEEDING THE CROWDS

Finding a lonely place in the Israel of Jesus' day was not always easy, especially around the populous western shore of the Galilean Sea. It has been estimated that in a country hardly larger than most American counties there were at that time more than two hundred cities with more than 15,000 inhabitants each. Jesus often had to go across the lake, five or six miles at the wider points, to find some solitude. As several disciples were fishermen by trade, transportation was no problem.

But on this occasion the enthusiastic crowds, knowing what Jesus intended to do, simply swept around the shore of the sea and were waiting for him on the other side. Instead of instructing the disciples to turn the boat about and head for the other side again, Jesus had such feeling for the people that he went ashore among them and continued healing their sick.

At the day's end, the disciples suggested that he send the people to get food. Doubtless they had a small store of food in their boat—Mark 8:14 indicates their habit of keeping a supply—but they were reluctant to take it out and begin eating in the presence of the crowds.

"Give them something to eat yourselves," said Jesus. "All we have," they replied, "is five loaves and two fish." "Let me have them," said Jesus. He blessed the loaves and fish and gave them to the disciples to distribute, and when everyone had eaten his or her fill, there were twelve basketfuls of scraps remaining.

The miracle is reminiscent of the Israelites' receiving manna from heaven as Moses led them through the wilderness. But, as Jesus is greater than Moses, the provision is much more abundant for those he feeds.

This was an important narrative among the early Christians, not only because Jesus was the new Moses but because the multiplication of the bread accorded so well with the Eucharistic meal which was the central rite of Christian fellowship. In a time when Christians sometimes met literally in the wilderness to avoid de-

57

tection, or at least in very private places, the story spoke eloquently of the way God daily provided their food for spiritual life.

> We are so inclined, Lord, to put our trust in programs organized for our future maintenance—in Social Security and insurance funds and savings accounts—so that we spend much of our present energy providing for tomorrow's needs. "In God We Trust," we say—and put the motto on our money. Help us to rediscover the meaning of freedom and spontaneity by depending on you for our daily bread. Through Jesus, who is sovereign of every wilderness place we can possibly inhabit. Amen.

Week VI: Tuesday

14:22–36 CHRIST AND HIS CHURCH

After feeding the people and sending them away, Jesus went up the hillside that swept duskily down to the sea. The average person would have done so in order to lie down and sleep after such a strenuous day. But Jesus went up to pray. He had learned long ago that prayer releases inner energies that restore the person even more than sleep.

Apparently Jesus had sent the disciples home for the night too, or else they had spent the night on the boat and then had put out very early in the morning to do some fishing. But the sea was rough and they were having difficulty. In the fourth watch, possibly as daylight was struggling to break through the storm, Jesus appeared to the disciples walking on the water. Shaking in terror, they thought they were beholding an apparition. Only his voice dispelled their fears.

Peter, always the most impetuous disciple, tried to walk to Jesus on the water. But the sight of the deep waves and the force of the wind made him falter, and the waters began to swallow him up. Swimmer that he doubtless was, he cried out for help. Reaching out and supporting him, Jesus chided him: "Why did you hesitate? How little faith you have!" And, when they were both in the boat, the wind suddenly died and the men all fell down exclaiming, "Truly you are the Son of God."

Imagine the situation in the early church's life to which a passage like this must have spoken. Persecutions had made survival difficult for the church. Jesus' reappearance was delayed beyond their expectations, just as he was late in coming to the disciples on the boat. Peter, who was probably already known as the chief spokesman of the church, had faltered badly at the time of the crucifixion. But Jesus had steadied him and helped him back into the boat. Clearly the exhortation to those in the church during this stormy period was to fall down and worship Jesus as the Son of God!

The remarkable picture in verses 34-36 is in keeping with such a passage. It is of the transcendent Christ passing through the crowds with people begging only to touch the hem of his garment. "And everyone who touched it," translates the New English Bible, "was completely cured."

> Lord, I am greatly moved by this picture of the early church and its worship. Grant that when the storms seem too much for us today we shall remember this passage and take heart. Through Jesus, who joins us in the troubled vessel. Amen.

Week VI: Wednesday

15:1-20 THE PARABLE OF THE UNRIGHTEOUS MAN

This material is closely related to Jesus' teachings in Matthew 5:17-48, where he said that he had not come to abrogate the Law of Moses but to fulfill it. The scribes and Pharisees in the passage are concerned once more with the failure of the disciples, who are nonobservant Jews, to keep the regulations or traditions which have become associated with the Law. The disciples do not perform the ritual lustrations before meals.

Stung by this persistent nettling over nonessentials, Jesus replies in two ways.

First, he reminds them that they themselves have *altered* the Law of Moses to make the commandment to honor one's parents avoidable, just as in Matthew 5:31–32 he reminded his audience that the law concerning divorce had been *weakened* to suit the contemporary legalists. In other words, they put their own traditions above the Law of God and teach as holy doctrines the commandments of men!

Second, Jesus gives his critics a brief parable: It is not what goes into the mouth that defiles a person but what comes out.

The disciples, uncomfortable with the tension that is building between Jesus and the legalists, ask him if he realizes he has angered his hearers. But he too is angry, and lashes back: "Let them alone; they are blind guides." Though they set themselves up as leaders of the people, they and the people will both fall into the ditch.

Peter, again the spokesman for the early church, asks for an interpretation of the parable. As in earlier cases, this is probably for the benefit of catechumens in the church of Matthew's age, who needed to understand the meaning of the saying. It is not the food entering the body that defiles it, says Jesus, but the talk coming out of it.

We recall that Paul had written to the Corinthians (8:1–13) about eating meat sold from pagan altars. In that instance Paul handled a similar question by saying that "food will not bring us into God's presence" but that he personally would eat no meat at all if it proved an offense to those whose faith was weaker than his.

Paul, of course, was dealing with a question *within* the community of believers, and so was inclined to be charitable. Jesus, on the other hand, was dealing with the incorrigible lawyers and Pharisees, whose scruples were of another order than those of the Christians who wished to abstain from meat given to idols. He was therefore inclined to do as he had instructed his disciples— shake the dust from his feet and abandon them to judgment.

Lord, those who meet about such things say that it is scruples over how the communion meal is to be taken that keep the major bodies of the church from uniting today. We are no better than the scribes and Pharisees, it seems, for we put our own traditions above fellowship and worshiping together. Save us from being blind guides of the blind. Through Jesus, who perennially rebukes our foolishness. Amen.

Week VI: Thursday

15:21–28   JESUS AND A FOREIGNER

If we are bothered by Jesus' tendency at this stage to define his mission in terms of Israel and not of the entire world, we must remember that Matthew's Gospel was written from a Jewish perspective to emphasize how Jesus had first fulfilled the prophecies regarding a Messiah for Israel. But this story very self-consciously represents Jesus as bringing benefits to the Gentile world as well.

The woman, a Canaanite, accentuates the Jewishness of Jesus by calling him Son of David. And she asks for so little—the crumbs that fall from the table. The Greek word used here for dogs, *kunaria,* specifically means small dogs—house dogs or lap dogs, as contrasted with the larger dogs that guard sheep or roam the fields. It is a gentle imploring that the woman makes.

Jesus cannot resist, and grants her request—her daughter is freed from the demonic spirit. The Gentile world begins in a small way to benefit from the coming of the Jewish Messiah!

From what small beginnings, Lord, sprang the riches that have come to the Gentile world from the Jewish Savior. My mind boggles at any attempt to enumerate your blessings to our culture. Freedom, peace, love, and all they mean in specific ways, are the gifts of your Spirit. We thank you through Jesus, who has broken down every wall that divided us, if we will only see that he has. Amen.

Week VI: Friday

15:29–16:12   WORRYING ABOUT BREAD

Again the story of the crowds and Jesus' compassion on them. Again the hesitance of the disciples—"We have only seven loaves and a few fishes." Again the blessing of what there was and the feeding with abundance in the wilderness. And again the nagging question of the Pharisees, "Show us a sign," with the cryptic answer that they were to have only the sign of the prophet Jonah.

"Beware," says Jesus to the disciples, "of the leaven of the Pharisees and Sadducees." Leaven was often used by rabbis as a symbol of evil and how quickly it permeates everything. But the poor dull disciples! They hear the word leaven and realize in an instant that they have failed to bring any bread with them, though there were so many basketfuls left over from the feeding of the four thousand. "He has caught us unprepared," they think.

"Don't you understand?" Jesus says. "I was speaking of the evil influence of the Pharisees and Sadducees, not of real bread."

The real point of the lesson may lie with the bread and not with the leaven, however; at least it appears so in the parallel passage in Mark 8:11–21. Twice Jesus had performed miracles in supplying bread for vast crowds—and here they were, a mere handful of disciples, worrying because they had no bread. Are we not prone to do the same—to forget the providence of God through the ages when we come to a moment of present need in our lives?

> Lord, I too am a dull disciple. I forget the many miracles that have sustained my life until this moment, and cry out as though lost because of some small need that must now be met. Help me to know there are no emergencies in your Kingdom—only opportunities to wait upon your generous hand. Through Jesus, whose lot it is to have dull disciples. Amen.

Week VI: Saturday

16:13–20 THE GREAT CONFESSION

There is lively debate about this passage. Some scholars think it is
an early attempt to bolster the papal authority of Peter by desig-
nating him as the foundation of the church and consigning to
him the keys of stewardship. Others insist that it is the confession
of Peter which is to be the foundation of the church.

Regardless of what the passage says about Peter, however, it
provides an important picture of Jesus. Several times in the Gospel, he instructs those he has healed not to tell anyone about
what he has done. Apparently he often worked among the crowds
with near anonymity. That this is so is enforced by his question
"Who do men say that the Son of man is?" and the answer the
disciples give, "Some say John the Baptist, others say Elijah, and
others Jeremiah or one of the prophets." Were it not for the attempt at secrecy, we should think this very strange; for all his
fame, Jesus was not widely known in his own right.

"Who do *you* say that I am?" he asks the disciples. "You are
the Christ, the Son of the living God," replies Peter. It is a
significant confession, registering what may have been only a
slowly maturing conviction on the apostles' part. In the boat, they
had recognized him as the Son of God (Matthew 14:33); but we
know that time sequences were often confused in the writing of
the Gospels, and there is some reason to suspect that the episode
in the boat may even have been at one time a postresurrection
narrative akin to John 21:4–8. Matthew apparently construed
Peter's confession as the first major recognition by the disciples of
the true scope of Jesus' work and ministry: He is not merely a
wonderful teacher and worker of miracles, he is the long-promised
Savior of the people!

Again Jesus counsels the disciples not to tell anyone who he really is, as though the secret must not yet be disclosed. And, from
this time on, he begins to prepare the disciples for the events of
the passion week and beyond, which now loom palpably close.

63

Lord, what a moment it must have been for the disciples when they moved like this from one level of recognition to another. They were surely filled with exultation. I am intrigued with the notion that it might be like that with me also—that the quality of my whole life could be suddenly altered by a deepened awareness of the meaning of Christ to my existence. Let it be, I pray, through him who reveals himself to faithful disciples. Amen.

WEEK VII

"Blessed is he who comes in the name of the Lord. . . . Save now! Save now in the highest!" (Week VIII: Wednesday)

He prayed that the dreadful hour of testing might simply go away, if possible—that he might be wrong about the series of events he saw rapidly building to a climax. (Week XI: Tuesday)

Week VII: Sunday

16:21–28 LETTING GO OF LIFE IN ORDER TO HAVE IT

From here on out, the shadow of the cross falls implacably across Matthew's account of Jesus' ministry. And how quickly Peter falls from the sublimity of the new order to the fear and hesitance of the old! He has barely made the great confession that Jesus is the Messiah, the Son of the living God, when Jesus speaks of his impending death and Peter counters with an oath to say, "No, Lord, this shall never happen to you!" He can no more fit the two things together—Messiah and death—than the crowds of unbelievers could. Jesus has cured the sick, made the blind see and the deaf hear, restored the leprous, cast out demons, and raised the dead. How can one with such power speak of dying a shameful death?

Again, we remind ourselves, the true time sequence meant little to those who wrote our Gospels. Perhaps Jesus had not yet taught the disciples the profound sayings which Matthew gathered into the Sermon on the Mount—especially the part about not being anxious but leaving life to God (6:25–34)—so that Peter's lack of understanding is permissible. Or, if Jesus had already given the sayings to the disciples, then the matter of the cross retrieved them and underscored them with new meaning.

"Get behind me, Satan!" says Jesus, rebuking Peter as furiously as he had a short time earlier congratulated him on his insight. "You are not on the side of God, but of men." Or, as the Jerusalem Bible translates it, "The way you think is not God's way but man's."

If the early church described in the book of Acts had taken a motto from the sayings of Jesus, this might well have been the one. "The way you think is not God's way but man's." For they no longer thought in the usual terms of cost, probability of success, and failure. They were like a people on fire for God, turning the world upside down, because everything seemed possible to them under God.

The secret, as Jesus explained to the disciples, is not to worry about self. It is in trying to grasp life and keep what we have that we lose everything; it is in living recklessly for God that we find everything! In the tidal wave of the Kingdom, only those who swim wildly with the tide will be saved—and the tide is already rising.

> *I want to take risks, Lord, and live unencumbered by selfish concerns. I would like even to own no property, but to wander the world as a servant. But I cannot help feeling responsible for my family. What am I to do about them? How can I be fully committed to you while caring for daily matters like orthodontist bills and fixing my son's bicycle? Help me to know the answer to this, Lord, because it perplexes me a lot. Through Jesus, whose commitment makes me feel guilty.* Amen.

Week VII: Monday

17:1–13 A FORETASTE OF THE NEW ORDER

This is an especially striking passage in the light of Matthew's theme that Jesus is the New Moses. The event apparently occurred during the Feast of Tabernacles, as Peter wanted to erect booths or tents for the three figures. The emphasis of Jewish thinking during this time was on the new age of the Messiah. The ascent of the mountain, the appearance of Moses and Elijah (who had been translated to heaven without dying), and the cloud representing the holy presence of God are all in keeping with this emphasis.

Jesus' face shines as Moses' did when he descended from Mount Sinai. The voice from the cloud, however, which is the same voice heard at Jesus' baptism in Matthew 3:17, announces that this is one greater than either Moses, who represents the Law, or Elijah, who represents the prophets. It is the beloved Son, which in Jewish thought is the closest identity a human being could have to God himself.

The entire event may be called an "eschatological theophany" —an appearance of God in a context suggestive of the way it will be in the Kingdom after the resurrection. The three disciples, who represent a kind of inner circle of authority not unlike that among the Qumran Essenes, are understandably frightened and excited by the scenario.

The presence of Elijah among the transfigured ones leads naturally to the disciples' question about the popular notion that he must return to earth before the age of the Messiah. Jesus indicates that the people of the age have already had their Elijah—John the Baptist—but failed to recognize him. And the reference to John is occasion for Jesus' reference to his own sufferings, which will be in dramatic contrast to the glory he has just shared in the transfiguration scene.

> *Mountains, light, the cloud—the symbolism of this passage is of height, loftiness, rarefication. It beckons me, Lord, from the tawdriness of my everyday concerns—from a cluttered desk, a messy laundry room, unpaid bills, a car in need of repair. Thank you for hallowing such moments, and for sending a light in my darkness.* Amen.

Week VII: Tuesday

17:14–20 WHEN FAITH IS TOO WEAK

This story must have been told for every lagging disciple in every age including our own. The situation in the life of the early church is not hard to imagine. After all the marvelous stories of Jesus' miracles of healing, and then of the disciples', especially in the book of Acts, some followers of the Way were distressed that they could not cast out demons, cure the sick, and raise the dead as their Lord and predecessors had. Did they not share the same power? Ah, says the Gospel, coming to their rescue, even the apostles failed on occasion because their faith was not strong enough.

Wc human beings are funny creatures. Faith transforms us. When we believe something strongly, we enter a new realm of possibility. I heard a man say that in an emergency his father had picked up the side of an automobile and held it while an injured person was removed from beneath the wreck; afterward he tried to lift it again and could not budge it. The crisis had propelled him into a new dimension of strength. Is it so hard to believe that miracles occur in the lives of those whose faith accepts miracles as natural?

> *Lord, moving mountains by faith is beyond my imagination. Maybe Jesus only exaggerated to make his point. I can believe in dramatic cures, telepathic messages, and superhuman strength. Help me to move from my present level of expectancy to one where such things are the rule and not the exception. Through Jesus, for whom miracles were a way of life.* Amen.

Week VII: Wednesday

17:22–27 A FISH STORY

Here, set against Jesus' prediction of his death and resurrection, this strange story. What can it mean? The intent is surely similar to that of the encounter between Jesus and the Pharisees in Matthew 22:15–22 about paying taxes to Caesar. The position of the early church seems consistently to have been pro-authority. Even though the government was corrupt and shared in the persecution of Christians, Christians were advised to pay their taxes, pray for their leaders, and live harmoniously in the temporal order. This passage involves the payment by Jewish Christians of the tax to maintain the temple in Jerusalem. After the Jews instituted new rules which deterred the Christians from participating in synagogue and temple worship, many Christians doubtless protested the temple tax assessments.

Jesus and his followers, who are giving their lives to God's work, should hardly be taxed to support a place dedicated to his worship. But, says Jesus in effect, we do not want to cause difficulty for those who merely enforce the rules, so we shall pay their tax. It is a rule of generosity for future generations, and much in keeping with the teaching of Matthew 5:41, "If a man in authority makes you go one mile, go with him two."

As for the fish story, which seems almost too fantastic to deserve a place in the Gospel, there is of course the possibility that it was symbolic and not realistic. We remember that the fish became a symbol for Christianity because the Greek word for fish, *ichthus*, was an anagram of the motto *Iesus Christos Theou Huios Soter*—"Jesus Christ, God's Son, Savior." Could the story have meant that the Christian community would pay the temple tax for its members? The early Christians, after all, did hold their goods in a common treasury.

> *It sometimes bothers me, Lord, to pay taxes to corrupt authorities. I feel that I could use the money much better for humane purposes. But Jesus never seemed to worry much about money; that wasn't what the Kingdom hinged on. Give me an open and generous spirit, I pray, that I may be more like him. Amen.*

Week VII: Thursday

18:1–14 GOD'S LITTLE ONES

This chapter constitutes another of the long discourses in Matthew which are collections of Jesus' teachings for the edification of the Christian community. To understand the full impact of this one, it is necessary to remember that one of the forces against which early Christianity had to contend was its own predecessor, Judaism. Throughout the Gospel, Matthew delineates the struggle between Jesus and the rabbinical system which was represented by the venerable rabbis who interpreted the Law and tradition. Much of Jesus' conflict with the scribes and Pharisees stemmed from the fact that his disciples were nonobservant Jews, neither learned in the Law nor committed to the traditions.

Now, in this brilliant passage, Matthew depicts Jesus as exalting not the aged figures of rabbis, growing more and more infirm as they master the arguments of earlier rabbis, but small children, who do not need the detailed refinements of the Law and tradition to mirror God's presence in the world. "Who is the greatest in the kingdom of heaven?" ask the disciples. And Jesus sets a child in their midst. "Unless you become like children, you will never enter the kingdom of heaven."

To the tradition-bound Jew, all of Jesus' followers are mere children, uneducated in the Law. Jesus passes from talking about actual children to these figurative children. "If anyone leads astray one of these little children who believe in me he would be better off thrown into the depths of the sea with a mill-stone hung round his neck!" (J. B. Phillips' translation).

Recall that, when Jesus denounced the cities that had refused his ministry, he said, "I thank thee, Father, Lord of heaven and earth, that thou hast hidden these things from the wise and understanding and revealed them to babes" (Matthew 11:25). It was a point Jesus made again and again in various ways. The Kingdom was a new creation; it could not be poured like new wine into old skins. It required fresh vigor and childlike imagination, untrammeled by too much devotion to mere tradition.

Perhaps Jesus anticipated criticism of the disciples and the Christian community. "Don't think too harshly of these little ones," he was cautioning in effect; "they have their guardian angels who look directly into the face of God. Of course they resemble sheep in their simple faith. But God has sent his Good Shepherd to find the sheep that the learned shepherds of Israel have disregarded. And there is great rejoicing whenever one of them is brought home to the Kingdom!"

> *Make me simple, Lord, as you are simple. Let my eye be sound and my entire body full of light. Calm my thoughts, that they fly not in a thousand directions. Still*

my impulses, that they may wait upon you as a sheep waits upon the help of its shepherd. Make me see your world fresh-washed and magical, like a child, and I shall glorify you this day. Amen.

Week VII: Friday

18:15–35 WHEN LITTLE ONES FALL OUT

How shall God's little ones deal with quarrels among themselves? Matthew here relates explicit teachings of Jesus on this subject. First there is patient exchange with the contentious person. Go to him or her and discuss the matter in question. If the person remains alienated, take one or two other Christians along and try again; perhaps he or she will be convinced upon hearing the facts from other perspectives. Should this not avail, then take the matter before the Christian community and let them deal with it. Perhaps the health of the entire organism is necessary to re-establish the health of the diseased tissue. But if the person remains obdurate even against the community, there is nothing left but to treat the person as an outsider.

The words spoken to Peter in the context of the great confession (Matthew 16:19) are repeated here: Decisions made in the community are decisions of the Kingdom as well. An ancient Jewish saying was, "Two that sit together occupied in the Law have the Presence among them." And, as the Christian community is formed by God's presence in the new creation, he is automatically involved in the decisions it makes.

Lest all of this seem too harsh, however, or the centrality of love in the community be lost, Matthew adds one more bit of teaching, about forgiveness. It is Peter, the head of the Christian community, who asks, "Lord, how often am I to forgive my brother if he goes on wronging me? As many as seven times?" Other Oriental laws of mercy said three times. Jesus replies, "I do not say seven times; I say seventy times seven." Such a number is

74

no longer literal, of course; it speaks of such depths of concern and forgiveness as cannot be measured.

There follows a parable on the Kingdom to remind every member of the community that he or she is there only by the grace of God. In one sense, it is a gloss on the phrase in the Model Prayer "Forgive us our debts as we forgive our debtors." We were all so far in debt—the poor character in this story was in by a king's ransom!—that there was no hope of ever paying. For us to be hard or unforgiving toward anyone else, then, over what in comparison can never amount to more than a beggarly amount, a few coins, is absurd; it proves we have not truly appreciated the magnitude of God's gift to us, and cannot in fact consider ourselves part of the Kingdom.

> *Lord, what a deep well of the Spirit this presumes! It reminds me with terrifying vividness of the shallow level at which I daily live. Give me a renewed consciousness of my freedom from debt, that I may respond to others always with exhilaration and joy. Through Jesus, who forgave others even from his cross. Amen.*

Week VII: Saturday

19:1–15 MARRIAGE MAKES ONE FLESH

Again Matthew takes up the greater-than-Moses theme, this time with regard to the law about marriage and divorce. Moses had said that a man could divorce his wife if he gave her a legal notification of dismissal. But Jesus, who said that he came to perfect the Law, not abolish it (Matthew 5:17–18), says that divorce is not permissible for any cause except unfaithfulness, regardless of Moses' saying. "It was because you knew so little of the meaning of love," says Jesus, "that Moses allowed you to divorce your wives! But that was not the original principle" (J. B. Phillips). In the creation, God ordained one wife for one husband; the two become one flesh. And in the new creation, it is clear, that is how Jesus intends it shall be.

In that case, say the disciples, it is better not to marry; marriage is too final a step to take. Not everyone is capable of making that decision, says Jesus; but whoever can ought to do so. Taken together with Paul's statement in 1 Corinthians 7:9, "It is better to marry than to be aflame with passion," this passage lays the foundation for clerical celibacy as it has been practiced through the ages.

Next, as if to underline the complexity of life when it must be regulated by law, Matthew turns once more to a picture of the children or little ones in their simplicity of lifestyle. Mothers have brought them to Jesus for him to lay hands on them and pray for them. The disciples, who characterize the insensitivity and male chauvinism of the age, and thus reveal much about the foregoing comments on marriage and divorce, try to drive them away. But Jesus stops them. He says again, "To such belongs the kingdom of heaven."

> Lord, this hard teaching on marriage would not be necessary if we had only learned the lesson about forgiveness in the preceding parable. We are selfish and demanding of one another without being mindful of our flawed characters or the enormity of our indebtedness to you. Help me to live as if my wife were the person in the parable who owed so little and I were the one who owed so much—for I truly think that is the way it is. Through Jesus, who commended love above everything. Amen.

WEEK VIII

Week VIII: Sunday

19: 16–30 PROPERTY AND THE KINGDOM

The French philosopher-playwright Gabriel Marcel once wrote a book called *Being and Having*, the thesis of which was that it is very difficult to *be* and to *have things* at the same time. Having inevitably gets in the way of being and begins to crowd it out.

That is largely the point of this famous story. The nearly perfect young man has only one major flaw: He is possessed by his possessions. When Jesus tells him he must part with his wealth in order to become a disciple, he is very sad. He knows what a grasp his riches have on him.

In a sense this passage is an extension of Matthew 6:19–34, where Jesus warned against trying to serve both God and money and counseled the disciples not to be anxious about the morrow. It illustrates our inability, when we have considerable possessions, to extricate ourselves from them and make radical commitments.

Perhaps the man is meant to pose a contrast between the esteemed Jew who strictly observes the Law and the little ones of the Kingdom. He has obviously done no wrong. In fact, he is bent upon doing good works. Matthew emphasizes this by slightly altering the material used by Mark. Mark has the man say, "Good teacher, what must I do to inherit eternal life?" (Mark 10:17). In Matthew he says instead, "Teacher, what good deed must I do, to have eternal life?" In ordinary Jewish eyes, the man was perfectly righteous, one of the blessed.

But Jesus pointed out, in effect, that the righteousness of the Jews before the Law was not sufficient. The Law was unable to measure the intent of the heart. It could not disclose the degree to which the man really worshiped his possessions, not God. The Kingdom, on the other hand, calls for total allegiance—the kind given by the disciples who have left their fishing boats to follow Jesus.

In the new creation, says Jesus, those who have forsaken selfish values for the Kingdom will have their full reward. Around him in his "heavenly splendour," as the New English Bible translates it, the disciples will sit on twelve thrones. Those who have endured calumny from the pious Jews because they are untutored in the Law and tradition will rule over their learned detractors. And all the little ones will be repaid many times for their faithfulness.

> *Lord, I confess that this passage makes me uneasy. I am too much like the rich man, who wanted to keep his property and be a disciple too. Help me to renounce my dependence on material things, so that I am not possessed by my possessions. Through Jesus, who found freedom through prayer and fasting.* Amen.

Week VIII: Monday

20:1–16 EQUALITY IN THE KINGDOM

This passage, which appears only in Matthew and not in Mark or Luke, is brilliantly placed after the story of the rich man and the disciples' discussion with Jesus. It cuts in two directions. On one hand, it is a warning to the legalistic Jews that God, because he is God, will treat the little ones of the Kingdom, the latecomers, as well as he treats them. On the other hand, it may also be a warning to the disciples that they are not to expect special consideration because they left all to follow Jesus at an early point in the Kingdom's coming, but will share it fully with all the little ones who enter late.

The point is—and this is always hard for work-oriented people to grasp—that the Kingdom is God's and *he* decides who will enter it and what their rewards will be.

Society and family have always tried to instill in us the feeling that we are worth what we *do*, not what we are. As children we grow up estimating our own value by external measurements—how hard we have worked, what we have accomplished, how much money we have made, and how we have improved our surroundings. Those of us who have done well by society's standards enjoy a glow of satisfaction and pride; those who have not feel a sense of guilt, as if they have not succeeded in life.

But God, being God, is not bound to or deceived by our standards of measurement. He gives the Kingdom to whomever he wills, the way a generous householder rewards the negligent servants as well as the diligent ones.

This is an important reminder in a Gospel which was written primarily to encourage the early Christians to a life of righteousness and faithfulness. As Jesus said to Peter in Matthew 19:26, the range of possibilities with God does not always coincide with ours. He is God, and above all laws—even the law of averages and the law of expectancy!

> Lord, this is far more hopeful to me than the last passage. I am not only a latecomer to the vineyard. I am terribly clumsy, and often step on tender plants or prune the wrong limbs. I also cherish the illusion that I am better than a lot of other workers. I am glad you are a God of mercy as well as a God of justice. Amen.

Week VIII: Tuesday

20:17–34 THE WAY TO BE GREAT

A journalist who had once desired to be an artist was thrilled with the assignment to interview the great Picasso. They had had their meal at a sidewalk cafe in Montmartre, the fabled artists' quarter of Paris, and their coffee cups were empty. The journalist kept glancing toward the waiter, attempting to get his eye. He seemed very annoyed. Noticing this, Picasso disappeared behind a curtain, emerged with a carafe, and provided a fresh cup for the astonished writer.

"Whoever would be great among you," said Jesus, "must be your servant." It was an important word for the Christian community, which has always had as much trouble with personal pride as any institution comprised of human beings.

Part of the irony of the request of the disciples and their mother, in Matthew's narrative, lay in its timing. Jesus had just spoken of his humiliating death and was on his way to Jerusalem where it would take place. We do not know whether the other disciples were angry with James and John because of the inappropriateness of such a request at such a time or because they too wished the places of honor. Jesus' speech to them seems to indicate the latter reason.

If Matthew had known the story related in John 13:1–11, of Jesus' taking a towel and washing his disciples' feet, he would surely have told it in this Gospel, for it illustrates even more graphically than allusions to the cross the meaning of the passage. True greatness shows itself in humility, not in pride of rank or place. Whoever would be first must become a slave.

> *How easy it is, Lord, to get by in a society where rank and place are easily fixed. Then all we have to do is the proper thing. But the Kingdom sweeps away all such defenses and leaves no rule but love. We are all servants, for your sake. I can only pray, "Your kingdom come."* Amen.

Week VIII: Wednesday

21:1–17 THE COMING OF THE KING

> Rejoice greatly, O daughter of Zion!
>   Shout aloud, O daughter of Jerusalem!
> Lo, your king comes to you;
>   triumphant and victorious is he,
> humble and riding on an ass,
>   on a colt the foal of an ass.

(Zechariah 9:9)

The last line of this poetic prophecy is known as a *parallelism*, and merely repeats in slightly altered form the last phrase of the line before it. Apparently some literal-minded translator did not understand this, and so altered the text as we have it in Matthew to picture an impossible thing: Jesus riding on two animals at once!

But the prophecy from Zechariah is an important background for comprehending the scene of Jesus' entry to Jerusalem at the beginning of the Passover week. No longer trying to keep his messiahship a secret, Jesus selects this image of the king riding a beast of burden as a way of announcing his mission. He comes as the one appointed by God to save his people.

As the crowd surges over the hill from Bethany and the Holy City comes into view, people along the way shout "Hosanna." The word is from Psalm 118:25–26 and is not a term of praise but a cry to "Save now!" The people do praise the Messiah by saying, "Blessed is he who comes in the name of the Lord." But the main shout that goes up from the crowds is "Save now! Save now in the highest!"

Jesus and the crowds apparently go straight to the temple, where Jesus overturns the tables of men who profiteer through exorbitant rates for currency exchange and through the sale of birds for sacrifice. The Gospel of John places the cleansing of the temple at the beginning of Jesus' ministry (John 2:13–22), and Mark chronicles it as belonging to the second day of the Passover week. But in Matthew's Gospel it is strategically located as Jesus' first act in this weeklong drama, perhaps underscoring his battle with the legalistic Jews. He cashiers those who traffic *legally* but *unspiritually* in the temple, and exalts it once again as a place of worship. In all the ancient prophecies, the temple had figured as the point of convergence for the new creation, with all nations flowing to it.

Similarly, the miracles of healing in the temple are symbolic of the new age, and the indignation of the chief priests and scribes to the cries of "Save now!" throws the conflict between old and new into sharp relief. Jesus has now seized the initiative. It is time for a culmination of the struggle between the old regime and the new.

*Lord, save us now from unspiritual systems and unin-
spired leaders. Enter the sacred places of world finance,
industry, education, and government where the poor are
daily cheated and defrauded. Take our part, and help us
to take the parts of others. Let every house become a
house of prayer. Through him who has come, still comes,
and is coming. Amen.*

Week VIII: Thursday

21:18–22 THE LESSON OF THE FIG TREE

This magical story is hardly in keeping with the Jesus we have
come to know in the Gospel. He does not go about performing
miracles for his own sake or because he is angry. If he did, then he
would in likelihood have yielded to the temptations described in
Matthew 4. Moreover, fig trees do not normally produce fruit
until early summer, and, even though the leaves were premature
on this particular tree, it does not seem reasonable that Jesus
would have cursed the tree for not bearing fruit out of season.

A clue to the meaning of the puzzling event may lie in verse 43
of this chapter, in the reference to "a nation that yields the proper
fruit." The fig tree probably stood for Israel. It was considered the
most important tree of the land, and was a symbol of fertility and
prosperity. Several pictures of the wrath of God in the Old Testament referred to his destroying the fig trees.

Jesus' cursing of the tree, then, was probably a parabolic saying
or even a parabolic action having to do with the failure of Israel.
It may have occurred at some other time and been drawn into the
chronology of Holy Week because of its dramatic picture of
God's wrath against the nation. Israel had put forth the leaves of
righteousness—the scribes and Pharisees had, that is—but had not
really brought forth the fruit of righteousness; her heart did not
truly belong to the Lord. Therefore God would curse the old Israel and she would never again have the chance to bear fruit.

Lord, forgive me for every time I have set forth leaves when I had no intention of bearing real fruit. Help me not only to be honest, but honestly to love you. Through Jesus, who was always what he appeared to be. Amen.

Week VIII: Friday

21:23–32 THE SON WHO PLEASES THE FATHER

It is Monday morning after the Great Entry on Sunday. When Jesus enters the temple, he is beset by the chief religious officers of the nation. "Who gave you the authority to act as you do?" they demand. The healings of the day before are still on their minds, but it was his act of riding into Jerusalem on the colt, announcing his messiahship, that has really jolted them. The cries of "Hosanna—save now!" probably ring yet in their ears. "What an upstart!" they must think. "How dare he come in here as though he were God's own anointed!"

They are shrewd old men. But Jesus gives them a taste of his own shrewdness. "Was John's baptism from God or from men?" They are political enough not to answer. So Jesus gives them a parable. Which is the father's delight, the son who promised a day's work and didn't give it or the son who said he wouldn't work but repented and did? They are practical fathers. There can be but one answer.

"Ah," says Jesus, drawing the noose, "the nonobservant Jews, whom you condemn, go into the Kingdom ahead of you, for they listened to John and repented. You are the sons who promised to go and did not."

How often, Lord, have I promised to enter the vineyard and did not. I meant to go, but the sun was hot or there were distractions on the way to the field. Now many less righteous than I go in ahead of me, because they acted promptly when they were asked to go. For-

give me, and let me go now, while there is yet time.
Through Jesus, who pierces me to the heart with his
stories. Amen.

Week VIII: Saturday

21:33–46 THE LANDOWNER'S SON

This remarkable parable is probably still a part of Jesus' answer to
the question "By what authority are you doing these things?" His
authority is that of a son—the final emissary sent from the landowner to claim the vineyard that was rightfully his.

As much as anything, the parable points to the violent death of
Jesus only four days hence. The wicked squatters hurl the son outside the vineyard and there murder him. Jesus, as the writer of
Hebrews is careful to point out in Hebrews 13:12, was crucified
outside the city walls of Jerusalem.

But the disenfranchised son becomes the foundation for a new
order. He is the stone rejected by the builders but reclaimed by
the architect and established as the chief cornerstone of the building.

There is no messianic secret. Jesus' meanings are all too plain to
the priests and Pharisees. They want to imprison him at once but
are afraid of the crowds who cried, "Save now!"

> *Lord, I like to think I would have been on Jesus' side*
> *against these selfish, evil leaders. But I am not so sure.*
> *There is that in me which sides with the powers that*
> *be—with law and order and due process. So I confess the*
> *possibility that I would have acted wrongly, and ask your*
> *forgiveness. Through the Son who lost his life.* Amen.

WEEK IX

Week IX: Sunday

22:1–14 THE WEDDING FEAST

Like the story of the landowner in Matthew 20:1–16, this parable is double-edged, so that it cuts both the self-righteous Jews and the false members of the Christian community.

First, the edge toward the observant Jews. From the beginning God, like the king in the parable, had given special invitations to the Jews. But they had not responded. Some were merely indifferent; others turned upon the servants who bore the king's message and brutally slew them. Finally there is no more time to send messages; the wedding feast is ready. Therefore the king redirects the invitation. This time it is to all the people in the streets, without regard to their backgrounds, stations in life, or anything else. These people pour into the dining hall until it is jammed with guests. Clearly this is a picture of the church or the visible kingdom. It is filled with people of many nations, who formerly have had no special relationship to the king.

But then comes the second edge of the story, the one directed toward the Christian community itself. The king enters the dining hall and finds a guest who has not even had the grace to dress for the occasion. The man is examined for this breach of etiquette and then cast out into the darkness. "Though many are invited," concludes the parable, "few are chosen."

The meaning for observant Jews is clear enough. But what does this portend for members of the Christian community? Taken in the context of Matthew's Gospel as a whole, it may be a warning to those who think they can be part of the banquet without conforming to the moral and ethical expectations of the host. Jesus, as the new Moses, expects his followers not only to fulfill the Law but to go beyond it. It would seem likely, then, that the king in the parable is not merely capricious in his behavior toward the guest without wedding clothes, but does what he does in righteous indignation at the disrespectful attitude shown by the guest.

Lord, I am tested by this parable. I like parties and banquets, and it appeals to me that the Kingdom is compared to a wedding feast. But I realize that I live in tattered garments—that my life is not so pure and gentle and self-denying as Matthew's Jesus asks. Help me to repent, and to find in Christ's righteousness a cloak for my own unseemliness. Amen.

Week IX: Monday

22:15–22 A CUNNING QUESTION AND A PIERCING ANSWER

It is not easy to deal with a question that is a trap and to emerge from it so victoriously as to leave the questioners dumfounded. Yet that it precisely what Jesus did in this instance.

The seriousness of the trap is underlined by the presence of the Herodians, supporters of Herod the Great, whom the Pharisees normally avoided. The fact that the Pharisees sent their disciples —an unusual case in the Gospels—probably means they avoided coming themselves. Because they considered Israel a theocracy and God their king, they felt religious scruples about the occupation of their country by foreigners and the payment of tribute money to a foreign emperor. Therefore they despised the Herodians, who curried favor with the Romans in order to maintain their local positions of influence, and would be opposed to any counsel from Jesus that it was lawful to pay taxes to Caesar. Moreover, if Jesus said that paying taxes to Caesar was lawful, they would surely spread the word and make Jesus unpopular with the crowds. The Herodians, on the other hand, would be unhappy if Jesus took the position that Roman taxation was unlawful, and would probably have him arrested on a charge of sedition. Either way, he was bound to lose.

But the clever questioners did not reckon with Jesus' resourcefulness. "Show me the money for the tax," he said. "Whose likeness and inscription is this?" It was Caesar's, of course. Every king or emperor, and some who only pretended to be, had coins struck in his image as a sign of his royalty. "Then give what is due to Caesar," said Jesus, "and give what is due to God."

It was a master stroke! Whatever bore the image of Caesar must belong to Caesar. But, by the same token, anything bearing God's image belonged to him. Man, made in the image of God, is not his own—and should be doing better things than trying to entrap good men with clever questions!

> Lord, most of us prefer asking you hard questions to giving you our love and loyalty. How tawdry it is of us, and what joy we are missing. Break through our clever games and show us life as it ought to be. Through Jesus, who knew what is due to whom. Amen.

Week IX: Tuesday

22:23–33 THE GOD OF THE LIVING

How intense the opposition to Jesus grows! First came the Pharisees and Herodians, strange bedfellows, with their malicious question. Now come the Sadducees, who are opposed to the Pharisees in most matters but see Jesus as a threat to the stability of their relationship to the Romans. The Sadducees were the upper-class ruling party of Israel, who numbered among themselves not only many prominent and educated families but the chief priests as well. They were strong adherents to the Pentateuch, the first five books of the Old Testament, and denied that the other writings were scriptural.

Because they found no mention of a resurrection in the Pentateuch, the Sadducees refused to accept the resurrection of the dead as a religious teaching. The Pharisees argued with them constantly about this, adducing texts from both the Pentateuch and later scriptures which they insisted clearly taught the doctrine of resurrection. For example, they sometimes cited Deuteronomy

31:16, which says, "And the Lord said to Moses, 'Behold, you are about to sleep with your fathers; then this people will rise' "—but which goes on to say, "and play the harlot after the strange gods of the land." The Pharisees tried to ignore the second part of the verse.

The picture, then, is of a group of men whose only interest in resurrection was polemical coming to ask Jesus a trick question about a matter in which he was on the side of the Pharisees. They cite the case of seven brothers who obeyed the Mosaic law and, each in turn as the other died, married the same wife, who followed the seventh in death. "In the resurrection," they ask, not even believing in resurrection, "whose wife will she be?" We can imagine the prideful mirth playing at the corners of their mouths.

"You are wrong," says Jesus, in effect—there is no mincing in his manner—"because you don't know either the scriptures or the power of God. You assume that life in the resurrection is limited to the forms of your present life. But it isn't! In the resurrection we become as free and marvelous as angels! There is no more need for legal contracts and institutions such as Moses gave for our protection now."

But Jesus is not through with that. He enters the ground where so many Pharisees have contended with the Sadducees and lost— the Torah itself. "Haven't you read what God himself said," he asks—" 'I am the God of Abraham, and the God of Isaac, and the God of Jacob'? The verb is present tense. You admit that God is living. Then Abraham, Isaac, and Jacob must be living too!"

> *Lord, I cannot help feeling that there is something cheap about such arguments, even for Jesus. I wish he had not been compelled to enter into such fruitless debates. But I suppose that is life, isn't it? We have to contend with ignorance and absurdity and misguided people; otherwise we have no compassion on the multitudes and leave them totally to their own devices. Help me to be more patient in dealing with cranks, as Jesus was. Amen.*

Week IX: Wednesday

22:34-40 THE TWIN PILLARS OF RELIGION

Mark's Gospel makes it clear that the lawyer who asked the next question of Jesus did so in a friendly manner because he respected the way Jesus had handled the earlier questions (Mark 12:28-34). In all sincerity the man inquires, "Which is the great commandment in the law?"

Jesus replies with the commandment most familiar to every Jew because it was part of the *Shema*, the opening sentence of every Jewish worship service: "You shall love the Lord your God with all your heart, and with all your soul, and with all your mind" (see Deuteronomy 6:5). That is all the man asked, but Jesus is not content to stop there. The trouble with the scribes and Pharisees was that they did stop there. Their religion was entirely vertical and without compassion. Therefore it became a charade, a mere posturing for effect. How much so will be evident in the next chapter of Matthew's Gospel, which is devoted to Jesus' seven indictments of the scribes and Pharisees.

Because the love of God is hollow and pretentious without horizontal relationships, Jesus immediately connects another commandment to the first: "You shall love your neighbor as yourself" (Leviticus 19:18). The *Shema* must be said in this light, for the two commandments are the twin pillars supporting all the Law and the prophets. Take either of them away, and everything collapses.

> *Lord, I catch myself rejoicing that I am not so stiff-necked or hardhearted as the Pharisees, and I realize that is a bad sign. If I loved my neighbor as myself, I would sympathize with their human frailty and pray for their salvation. Forgive me for defining my neighbor in such a way as to make my loving easier, and grant that my understanding of religion may rest more solidly on genuine care for others. Through Jesus, whose love for you and his neighbor led him to a cross. Amen.*

Week IX: Thursday

22:41–46 MORE THAN THE SON OF DAVID

The Pharisees are apparently stunned to silence by Jesus' answer about the commandments, so Jesus follows with a question of his own. "Whose son is the Messiah?" he asks. It is a simple question. "David's," they answer, because "Son of David" is the most common messianic title. The scribes and Pharisees have heard the crowds calling Jesus Son of David, and know he is aware that they are thinking this.

"What about Psalm 110:1," says Jesus, "where David says, 'The Lord said to my Lord, sit at my right hand'?" The reference, it is agreed, is to the Messiah. "If David calls him Lord, then isn't he more than a mere son?"

If the hearers were stunned before, now they are awe-stricken. Have they heard correctly? Does Jesus claim to be more than a man? There will be no more badgering questions. The next questioner, in fact, will be the high priest who examines Jesus for blasphemy (Matthew 26:57–68).

> *This must have been a high moment, Lord—a daring moment. I appreciate the drama of it because I know its awful consequences. Help me to follow him whom you have named Lord, and who at the end claimed the title.* Amen.

Week IX: Friday

23:1–12 THE TROUBLE WITH THE PHARISEES

We must recall again that as Matthew wrote his Gospel the Christian community was still struggling to establish its identity over against Judaism. This entire chapter constitutes another collection of sayings gathered under a special heading. There is no

93

way of knowing for sure that all the sayings were given at once; probably they were not. Matthew has grouped them into an introduction, seven woes or indictments, and a conclusion.

The admonishment to do what the scribes and Pharisees say, but not what they do, is interesting. It is not the Law that is so bad, nor even the scribal additions to it, but the attitude with which the scribes and Pharisees approach them. They have set themselves up as an elite corps of men to make heavy burdens for others to bear.

Actually the Pharisees had existed for only a couple of centuries by Jesus' time. Their name meant "the Separated Ones." They dedicated themselves to obeying all the laws and regulations extrapolated by the scribes from the Torah—so many that they filled more than fifty volumes! Being a Pharisee was therefore a full-time job; one had to study and work constantly at perfecting himself.

As Jesus saw, such zealousness was often misplaced. Separation became a source of pride to many Pharisees, and they became unbearable tyrants toward others who were less perfect than they. Their sin was not their devotion to religion but their lack of charity toward others.

"They are self-centered," said Jesus, "and pretend to honor God when what they really do is honor themselves, for God takes no honor in uncharitable worship. They like to have the highest places at public events because they are regarded as holy men, and they enjoy being called Teacher because they can quote so many fussy laws. Don't ever aspire to that. Let the titles go. You have one Teacher, one Father, one Master—don't set up others."

The church, of course, has been as clever as the scribes at getting around this admonition. We have popes, bishops, archbishops, rectors, reverends, right reverends, pastors, associate pastors, canons, deacons, elders, deans, and a dozen other titles to which Christians can approvingly aspire. But Jesus counseled against being caught up in such peripheral matters. In words reminiscent of his counsel to the disciples when James and John wanted the places of honor in the Kingdom (Matthew 20:26–28), Jesus said that true greatness lies through service to others, not through self-exaltation.

Lord, it is hard to serve others without thought of re-ward, and to love when love is not returned. Yet Jesus has asked this of us, and has done as much himself. Help me to strive for this point of selflessness in my life, that I may enter the joy of the Kingdom. Amen.

Week IX: Saturday

23:13–39 THE SEVEN WOES

It is hard to imagine the Jesus of the Beatitudes giving vent to such invective as marks this long passage. As William Barclay says, "It is seldom in literature that we find so unsparing and sustained an indictment as we find in this chapter." But we must remember, to understand it, that the scribes and Pharisees, more than anyone else, were poisoning the spiritual wells of Israel. And they, more than anyone, were trying to block Jesus' ministry to the people. The last verses of this chapter indicate a man on the verge of tears in his frustration to minister to the holy city. Perhaps they are the best clue of all to the outrage he felt against the ever-present religious bigots who had stoned the prophets in earlier ages and would crucify him in this one.

The description of the scribes and Pharisees is devastating: They will not enter the Kingdom of heaven themselves and they keep others from entering; they scour the world to make disciples, and then make torments of the disciples' lives; they keep all the fine points of the Law and miss the most important ones; they make themselves appear holy but are filled with corruption; they speak of honoring the prophets but are as hungry to murder prophets as their fathers were.

No wonder the formula for the woes begins each time, "Woe to you, scribes and Pharisees, hypocrites!" There would be no more stinging indictment for persons who held religion in high esteem. The word hypocrite in Greek originally applied to an actor who carried a large mask in front of him as he played his part, one that could easily be seen by the whole audience. That was precisely the way Jesus pictured the Pharisees—they were men wearing oversized masks!

> *Lord, save us all from the burdens of other people's religious expectations, and save them from ours. Let us be content to meditate on our own faults and spend no time accusing others. And grant to each of us a sense of the positive meaning of faith, in order that we may not lose touch with you through expressions of negativism. Through Jesus, whose religion was so healthy-minded that he knew how to deal with scribes and Pharisees. Amen.*

WEEK X

"Teach us the ways of him who prayed even for those who nailed him to a cross." (Week XII: Monday)

"O Lord, renew the sense of your presence among us, that your teachings may gain new purchase on our imaginations." (Week XII: Saturday)

24:1–14 THE GOSPEL FOR THE WORLD

This chapter is another of Matthew's collections of teachings drawn from various times in Jesus' ministry and assembled because they all relate to a particular theme. The theme in this case is difficult times.

The first saying, verses 1–2, may have occurred on one of the first visits Jesus made to Jerusalem with the disciples, because we have the disciples coming to him in amazement, like gawking tourists, to point out the temple buildings. Although the temple was hardly large by contemporary standards, it probably appeared gigantic to these country visitors, and it was certainly magnificent, for it was constructed of white marble overlaid with gold. When Jesus said that not a stone of it would be left standing, he was apparently not referring to the destruction of the temple in A.D. 70, for Josephus said that the temple was then destroyed by fire. Possibly he was making a general statement about the failure of the religion of the scribes and Pharisees (remember the "woes" of chapter 23)—the temple, as the symbol of that religion, was doomed to eventual ruin.

The next saying, placed on the Mount of Olives, which was traditionally associated with the messianic age, is in answer to a question about signs of the *parousia*, or Second Coming, and the end of the age. Jesus describes the difficult early years of the church, when Christians were persecuted for their faith and there was much confusion in the world. Perhaps the most chilling part of the description is the warning that "men's love will grow cold." But the gospel will be preached to all the nations, and then—the time is not specified—the end will come.

> Sometimes, Lord, I think this is the age when love has grown cold. People are so insecure and frustrated that they quarrel, cheat, and gouge one another without respect to either the morality or the love of Christ. It is a

time of distress and unhappiness. Help me to be a res-
ervoir of strength and gentleness to others this day, and
to give my life in love as Jesus did. Amen.

Week X: Monday

24:15–31 A TIME OF CONFUSION

It would take far more space than we have here to begin to untangle the references of these verses, some of which are to the destruction of Jerusalem and some to the end of the age. The "desolating sacrilege" of verse 15 is clearly a reference to Daniel 9:27, 11:31, and 12:11, where the prophet reflected on the desecration of the temple by Antiochus Epiphanes, king of Syria, who erected an altar to Zeus there and sacrificed swine on it. Apparently Jesus is warning the Christians to flee from the city when a foreign ruler does this again, for it is a sign of the collapse of all things.

In a time of such confusion, there will naturally arise many false messiahs who assume, because they too can see the signs of the end, that they are God's intended leaders. Even some of the chosen community will be deceived by them. "But don't listen to them," says Jesus. "Remember what I have told you. When the Son of man really appears again, it will not be in a corner, in some limited way; he will be seen from east to west, like the lightning."

As for verse 28, it is apparently a proverb. The word for eagle may also be translated vulture, as most modern translators have shown. Taken thus, it probably applies to the appearance of false messiahs, who, like vultures, will gather over the body of civilization.

The whole universe is seen to collapse in the terrible Day of the Lord. But in the midst of the desolation will come the one who is to rule the new creation. His angels will fly all over the heavens, gathering the chosen together.

Lord, I get lost in all this business of signs and predictions. I am also bothered by those who don't see its poetic character, but insist on counting the days and weeks until the end. Help me to keep what is primary in all this, though—the vision of Christ as sufficient to all his little ones, whatever comes in the world—and not lose it with all of the unsettling language. Amen.

Week X: Tuesday

24: 32–51 MORE SAYINGS OF THE END

There are obvious signs of the collapse of all things, says Jesus. The intelligent person learns to read such signs, the way he or she knows, when the fig tree puts out its leaves, that summer is near. But there is no way of knowing the exact time, so it is important to continue working and living as one normally does.

We know from Paul's writings that some Christians, expecting the imminent end of the world, simply quit working. Foreseeing this possibility, Jesus gave the parable of the servant who, when his master suddenly appears, is faithfully setting food before the other servants. The servant who says that because the master has been gone so long he will surely not arrive today, and therefore neglects his duties, will be punished with the hypocrites—and we remember that the formula for the seven woes of chapter 23 was "Woe to you, scribes and Pharisees, *hypocrites.*"

Lord, make us faithful servants to do the small things that are important in the daily affairs of people and save us from any tendency to resign our care for others. Through Jesus, who never asked to be waited upon. Amen.

Week X: Wednesday

25:1–13 THE JOY OF READINESS

It is possible that this parable is not about the return of Christ at all, but about the coming of the Kingdom to the Jews, and was attracted to its present textual position by its eschatological flavor. If this is so, then Israel was the bride of the story, and the ancient manuscripts may be correct which add "and the bride" at the end of verse 1.

The custom was for maidens to attend the bride, not the bridegroom, and then to accompany the two as the groom took the bride from her parents' house to his. If Israel was the apparent bride, then the maidens were the religious leaders responsible for seeing her delivered to the Messiah. Some of them, because of the hard intertestamental period and the failure of the Messiah to appear, had turned their thoughts to other things and simply were not prepared for the Kingdom when Jesus came among them with his message.

Verse 13 may have been at some point a textual addition, though not an unworthy one, for the theme of watchfulness is always applicable in spiritual matters.

> *Lord, we are all inclined to slothful spirits. Our sensibilities become dulled and we miss many opportunities each day of seeing your advent in our lives. Resensitize us, we pray, until we live on tiptoe, expecting you at every moment.* Amen.

Week X: Thursday

25:14–30 MISJUDGING THE MASTER

Once more we have a parable subject to two interpretations. Jesus very possibly told it with the Jewish religious leaders in mind: the scribes and Pharisees were the one-talent servants who had been mere niggardly guardians of what had been given them in the Law. But Matthew's placement indicates that the early church saw in the parable a challenge to faithful living in its own time, and indeed in that sense it is timeless.

The servant's error was his misreading of the master's nature. He had seen only half of that nature—the tendency of the master to be a zealous farmer, gathering in hay and grain even in places where it sprang up wild and had not been cultivated. He mistook this for miserliness, when in reality it indicated imagination, risk, and resourcefulness.

This certainly would have applied to the legalistic religious leaders of Jesus' day. They looked upon the religion God had given as something to be carefully guarded and restricted—hence their impossibly elaborated system of rules and taboos. They had completely overlooked the real dynamic of Judaism, which was able to produce John the Baptist, Jesus, and of course Christianity itself.

> *Lord, there is something in all of us that loves rules and prescriptions. We feel safer if we can take the measure of things and assign them to well-defined categories. But your Spirit is more than we are able to express in formulas and regulations. You transcend our definitions and dogmas; you elude our finest theologies. Help us not to be caught as the third servant was, with spirits timid and fearful. Let us ride the wild waves of the Kingdom's coming, like surfers joyous and unafraid, because we trust him who has gone before us.* Amen.

Week X: Friday

25:31–46 THE CENTRALITY OF THE "LITTLE ONES"

Few passages in Matthew's Gospel are more moving than this one. It represents the culmination of centuries of longing for justice; and, when justice is done, it is seen not in terms of mere legalistic righteousness, such as the scribes and Pharisees were interested in, but of care for all of God's little ones.

We tend, after centuries of habit, to read the saying as applicable to some distant future. But when the disciples first heard it, it was surely clear to them that the goats of the parable were the scribes and Pharisees, the strictly observant Jews, who had put heavy burdens on the common people and had not really cared about their salvation (compare Matthew 23:4). The sheep, on the other hand, were the little ones of the Kingdom. The Messiah-king identified with the little ones, and thus brought judgment on the others.

There is no sharper warning to religious people in any generation than this parable, for it reminds us of man's perennial tendency to regard the poor, the unattractive, and the powerless as outsiders in the human community; and such an attitude always carries its own judgment in God's created order.

> Lord, I think of the person I most despise, and of the reasons for that. Is it wrong of me to make such judgments? Am I in effect pronouncing judgment on myself, because I have not loved as I was told to? I fear it is so. Forgive me—as I try to accept the person I despised. Amen.

Week X: Saturday

26:1-13 A BEAUTIFUL ACT

Here, set between pieces of information about the gathering storm that will break over Jesus before the week is out, is a story of tender devotion which has, as Jesus predicted, been told all over the world.

Probably the action occurred in the evening, as it was in Bethany and Jesus spent his days in Jerusalem a few miles away. Jesus and the disciples were resting in the home of Simon the leper—apparently one of the persons Jesus had healed. John's Gospel indicates that the woman with the jar of ointment was Mary, the sister of Martha and Lazarus, who also lived in Bethany.

With her loving intuition, Mary perceived the tragic meaning of Jesus' predictions concerning his conflict with the authorities. With characteristic generosity, she came to him in Simon's home bearing the vessel of ointment which she had probably been saving for her own and her family's anointment after death. It was a very costly substance, worth as much as an average man might earn in a year. Either in sympathy or in loving protest of the way Jesus was about to spend himself, Mary poured the entire amount of ointment on his head, so that it ran profusely through his hair and into his clothing. The room was immediately filled with the sweet, thick odor of death.

The disciples, who had been sensitized to the needs of the poor, were outraged. (John's Gospel, written later, pins the blame for their outburst on Judas the traitor.) Why wasn't the ointment sold for the benefit of the poor, if she wanted to honor Jesus?

But Jesus commended the woman. She had seen something important: They were in the presence of the Lord of the new creation. There were other resources for the poor—and this example was never intended to gainsay the importance of caring for the poor. But Mary had prepared the King for his burial. Her recognition of the situation was greater than the disciples', and her deed would always be associated with the community's proclamation.

Lord, increase in me the capacity for spontaneous acts of generosity. Let me forget self and use my substance for others, as this woman did. I do not wish to forget the poor; but neither do I wish to lose the ability to do lavish, beautiful things for those around me. Through Jesus, who understood and approved. Amen.

WEEK XI

26:14-25 THE PERFIDY OF JUDAS

Sometimes even strong men break under the pressure of relentless conflict. They are not innately bad or prone to misjudgment; it is just that something snaps and they do unpredictable things, things absurdly out of keeping with their usual character.

It may have been that way with Judas. Surely something in him had recommended him to Jesus as a disciple. But in the constant battle with the authorities in Jerusalem he reached a point where he couldn't take it any longer. Maybe he thought Jesus was wrong to speak of dying instead of fighting; or, as some have suggested, perhaps he thought he could provoke a revolution in which Jesus would emerge victorious.

At any rate, he agreed to deliver his master into the hands of the chief priests for thirty pieces of silver, which according to Exodus 21:32 was the price of a slave. Ironically, Judas enslaved himself and vilified his name forever in this transaction. The name Judas has ever since been synonymous with treachery and deceit.

How did Jesus know? There were surely many telltale signs in Judas' behavior. One of them, we now suspect from our knowledge of the Qumran materials, was his dipping his hand with Jesus into the bowl of bitter herbs which was part of the Passover meal. The rule in the Essene community at Qumran was that people dipped their hands in the bowl in hierarchic order; that is, in the sequence of their statuses. Judas' dipping his hand with Jesus suggests a breach of etiquette on his part—as though he suddenly felt equal with the Master.

> Lord, there is Judas in me too. I bristle with self-importance and confidence in my own opinions. Sometimes I think I know better than you what I need or should do. At such times, I crowd the bowl by dipping as you dip. Forgive my terrible impertinence; help me to live humbly and devotedly, that I may not betray you. Amen.

26:26–35 THE FIRST SUPPER

A friend has suggested that the meal which Jesus ate with the disciples is improperly referred to as the Last Supper. Why shouldn't it be called instead the *First* Supper? It was, after all, the beginning of a tradition which has been so central to Christianity through the years as to make it the primary sacrament of the community.

But why, in light of this primacy in the community, did Matthew spend so little time describing it? In the Gospel of John it is accorded several chapters. Perhaps Matthew was more concerned with the actual enactment of the passion story than with its mere symbolization. All Christians knew the meaning of bread and wine. He was interested in the human drama being played out beyond the table, in Judas and Peter and Caiaphas and Pilate and all the others whose stories held so much significance for the entire community. Thus he hastens on from the bare fact of the Supper's institution to describe Peter's protestation of faithfulness —a protestation we know to be ill-fated.

Ironically, the hymn which Jesus and the disciples sang before going out was probably Psalm 118, which contains the words:

> With the Lord on my side I do not fear.
>> What can man do to me?
> The Lord is on my side to help me;
>> I shall look in triumph on those who hate me.
> It is better to take refuge in the Lord
>> than to put confidence in man.
> It is better to take refuge in the Lord
>> than to put confidence in princes. (6–9)

But Peter and the other disciples apparently forgot what they had sung.

Their guilt is my guilt, O Lord. I too betray you, in a thousand small betrayals. I disappoint children who have looked to me expectantly; I fail my elders, who desire my care and attention; I give less than my best to my friends, who had reason to hope for more. If they are your little ones, Lord, then I have fallen short of your wishes too. Forgive me and help me to do better. Through him who loved even those who let him down. Amen.

Week XI: Tuesday

26: 36–46 PRAY TO BE SPARED THE TESTING

Professor David Daube has reminded us of a rule among the Jews that whenever one of the group celebrating the Passover fell asleep—not merely dozed but fell into deep sleep, so that he could not answer a question—it was the end of the celebration. This rule explains the puzzling way Jesus kept returning to the disciples as he prayed—he did not want the Passover celebration to come to an end.

There is great pathos in this picture of Jesus, deeply saddened by the betrayal of Judas and the impending events of the next few hours. It was entirely natural for him to seek comfort in prayer, for it had been his discipline at earlier times to spend many hours in prayer. Now the prayer had a cruciality about it that it had perhaps never had before.

What did Jesus pray at this time? He prayed that the dreadful hour of testing might simply go away, if possible—that he might be wrong about the series of events he saw rapidly building to a climax.

He also instructed the three disciples, Peter, James, and John, to pray a similar prayer for themselves. But of course they did not. They were tired and did not realize the seriousness of the hour, so they failed to pray as they were bidden. And with what enormous consequences! Jesus came out of Gethsemane refreshed in spirit and ready to endure the worst the authorities could do to him. If the disciples had prayed, they too might have been refreshed, and, instead of fleeing, they might have died by Jesus' side. It is a tremendous thing to ponder, isn't it? Prayer can actually get us into trouble; or it can keep us there if we are already in it!

> *Lord, too often my prayers are mere recitations of shopping lists. I do not use them as opportunities for listening to you and learning what I should be doing with my life. Therefore I live wastefully and in needless desperation. Help me to take prayer more seriously, and not to fall asleep. Through Jesus, who was crucified. Amen.*

Week XI: Wednesday

26:47–56 NOT WITH SWORDS LOUD CLASHING

The irony of verse 25 is continued here as Judas calls Jesus Master and kisses him. It was considered impudent of a disciple to kiss his master before the master had first kissed him, and Judas once more demonstrated his feeling of equality with Jesus. In light of this, it is possible that Jesus' calling him "friend" was intended sarcastically, not seriously.

John 18:10 tells us that the unnamed disciple who drew his sword was Peter. The fact that a mob had followed the chief priests and elders to the site enhances the possibility that this action was very significant. It might easily have signaled the eruption of local warfare, for probably many in the crowd as well as in the entire city were prepared to follow Jesus in an armed rebellion.

There were surely in the early Christian community, too, many who felt that Christians should do more to defend themselves against imprisonment and persecution. Why not train secret militia to offset the power of the corrupt authorities?

The example of Jesus, and his words about not taking up the sword, have had great influence through the ages on the Christian attitude toward violence. In our own time, they were persuasive to

Mahatma Gandhi and Martin Luther King, Jr., both of whom influenced millions of oppressed people.

It is the royal demeanor of Jesus here that causes us to question his use of power for selfish purposes in the stories of the fish with money in its mouth (Matthew 17:27) and the withered fig tree (Matthew 21:18–22). Such tales are simply incongruent with the behavior of one who offered himself so gracefully to his own executioners.

> *Lord, we understand so little of the nature of power—that it finally harms those who would use it selfishly against others. We are always drawing our swords for this or that reason, and attacking the enemies without. Help us to know what enemies lurk within, and to submit ourselves to you for more perfect cleansing. Through him who resisted the impulse to summon angels in a frightening moment. Amen.*

Week XI: Thursday

26:57–68 THE JUDGMENT OF THE OLD MEN

The Romans, as Matthew made abundantly clear, were only incidental accessories in the death of Jesus. It was the religious leaders of the Jews, from first to last, who resented his style of ministry, his popularity with the poor, and his way of besting them in argument. There is no mention in this chapter of a Roman soldier's having been present in the capture of Jesus, despite the danger the mob scene constituted to the civil peace. It was all the work of the Jewish authorities. And now the same authorities proceed with their council meeting to try Jesus.

As the Sanhedrin or Council of Elders had no power to impose the death penalty except in cases of Gentile violation of the sacred area of the temple, it is probable that they commenced by trying to find Jesus guilty of some seditious act which they could then report to the Roman procurator. But failing this, apparently because of confusion among the false witnesses, they finally established a religious accusation against him, that of blasphemy. When Jesus admitted to being the Son of God, the high priest, following a custom prescribed for such situations, tore his robes. The elders, shocked by the brazenness of the accused, declared that he deserved to die. Leviticus 24:16 prescribes death by stoning as the punishment for blaspheming. Perhaps because they lacked the authority to inflict the penalty they desired, the elders broke into a frenzy of petty retribution, spitting on Jesus, slapping him, and taunting him.

As Jesus had said about them, they were devoid of love, the absence of which turned their professed love of God into a demonic caricature of true religion. They acted out, in this wild scene, the very portrait of them he had painted.

> *Lord, was ever any scene more chilling than this? What terrible things men do in the name of religion, truth, and honor! Save me from participating in such assassinations. Let me suffer with the accused rather than be a party to such evil judgments—even when all that is involved is petty gossip and not a trial such as this. Through Jesus, who always befriends victims of injustice. Amen.*

Week XI: Friday

26:69–75 THE FALL OF THE ROCK

Why was the story of Peter's defection so much more important than those of the other disciples, who also ran away? Why, indeed, but that by the time the Gospels were written it was Peter who had clearly emerged as the most significant figure in the Christian community. Because he was the leader, the story of his faltering was all the more engaging to the community. It reminded them of the utter frailty of the human foundations of their movement. The man whom Jesus had called the Rock had proved unstable in a critical moment. He had slept when Jesus told him to watch and pray, and then he had lacked the courage to confess his relationship to Jesus in the very courtyard of the enemy!

Later, at Pentecost, Peter would be fired with courage and would excoriate the same elders for having crucified Jesus. He would become known for his dedication to the community, and legend would represent him as being crucified upside down because he did not deem himself worthy of dying as his Lord had.

Imagine what encouragement this biography would have been to frightened, hesitant Christians everywhere. Peter, the big fisherman, had once hesitated too. But then he had wept in repentance and become the rock Jesus called him to be. Surely every Christian can respond in the same positive manner to his or her own former acts of defection and become doubly responsible in the Kingdom!

> *I am grateful, Lord, for what the snatches of Peter's biography have meant to me in my own Christian pilgrimage. It is good to have someone imperfect to relate to, for there are times when I am discouraged by my own faithlessness and betrayal. Accept my repentant spirit for every time I have denied the impulse to witness to your presence, and help me to show fruits of that repentance as Peter did. Through him who stands forever in the dock as we struggle in the courtyard. Amen.*

Week XI: Saturday

27: 1–10 THE REPENTANCE OF JUDAS

How difficult it is to call back a word or an action once directed against another human being. Judas learned this bitterly in the case of his betrayal of Jesus. Perhaps he thought Jesus would best the elders in a showdown. But when he learned that the elders had condemned Jesus and sent him to Pilate, the raw, ugly truth of what he had done hit him with sickening impact. Hurrying back to the chief priests, he tried to undo what he had done. Failing that, he hurled the blood money on the floor of the temple and left despondently. Whether he took his life that very morning, dying when Jesus did, or later, the record does not indicate. It only tells us that the money, because it was tainted by blood, was used to buy a burial site for strangers, fulfilling a prophecy from Zechariah 11:12–13 (not Jeremiah, as the manuscripts have it). Thus the memory of Judas would always be associated with strangers and outcasts—people who had no friends to bury them.

> *Lord, what a lonely position Judas was in. I pray now for all persons who contemplate suicide. Help them to know that somewhere, somehow, someone cares for them. Through Jesus, who was Judas' friend. Amen.*

WEEK XII

Week XII: Sunday

27:11–26 A STRONG MAN BEFORE A WEAK MAN

"Are you the king of the Jews?" asked Pilate. It was an important question, legally at least. Apparently the chief priests and elders had translated the term Messiah that way for Pilate when they brought Jesus before him. Pilate was, after all, head of the Roman occupation, and would take the matter more seriously if he thought Jesus was after the throne of Herod; that would mean insurrection and trouble.

But Pilate was canny. He listened to the old men of Israel snapping off charges against Jesus, and he watched Jesus waiting silently before them. He knew that the old men did it all for envy —that they feared this strange young prophet with such deep ways.

Pilate was in a ticklish situation. He believed the man innocent. His wife had even had a dream about him, and warned Pilate not to have anything to do with him. But the situation was explosive. The elders could make trouble for him among the people and with his superiors in Rome.

So Pilate did the discreet, political thing—and earned infamy as a result. Now we class him with all those persons who consider career and influence above right moral action; and Jesus, who was willing to die for a righteous cause, is revered even by non-Christians throughout the world.

> Lord, grant that I never lose touch with myself to the extent that I could wash my hands of anyone whose well-being depended on me—even someone I knew as fleetingly as Pilate knew Jesus. Let me be prepared instead to go to a cross of some kind, if necessary, in behalf of truth, honor, probity—the things that matter. Through Jesus, who would have acted differently if he had been in Pilate's place. Amen.

27:27–44 JESUS AND THE CARNIVAL

Bruegel the Elder once painted a crucifixion scene that captured the carnival-like qualities of that awful day. It is called *The Procession to Calvary*. It shows Jesus being led out of the city ahead of a mob of people who are excited by the smell of blood and violence. Someone is turning a somersault. A boy is pole-vaulting over a mud puddle. Two men are already on distant crosses. Jesus has fallen beneath his. In the lower left quadrant of the painting, a tug of war is going on between Simon of Cyrene's grim-faced wife and the soldiers who want Simon to help Jesus with the cross. Simon is in the middle, being held by his wife and pulled by the soldiers. Most of the people are utterly indifferent to the exhausted figure of Jesus. They are simply out for a good time.

Bruegel has seen what is apparent in this passage—the cruel and ugly side of humanity that takes pleasure in the pain of others or enjoys the defeat of a famous personality. It is not a pleasant thing to behold. In fact, it makes one ashamed that people could behave in such calloused ways.

But we remember that Jesus came as the Messiah of the new creation, and creation always means pain and suffering as order is wrought out of chaos. Here was the climactic moment in his struggle with the forces of evil, and evil was making its strongest play.

> *Lord, there is bloodlust in us that makes us take pleasure in other people's misfortune. Forgive this dark streak and turn us to tenderness; let mercy temper justice and love replace vengeance. Teach us the ways of him who prayed even for those who nailed him to a cross. Amen.*

Week XII: Tuesday

27:45–56 GIVING UP THE SPIRIT

When the crucifixion was over and the various stories about it were assembled, it was apparent that things were occurring at two different levels.

At one level, the carnival level, the crowds gaped at the spectacle of a man dying. Once, when Jesus was reciting Psalm 22, a psalm of both despair and victory, they thought they heard the name Elijah on his lips, and said he was calling the prophet. Elijah was believed to come to the aid of the righteous when they suffered. Someone ran to get a sponge and poured cheap wine on it and raised it on a stick to Jesus. The man may have meant well. But the others told him to wait and see if Elijah really would come to help the dying man. Then Jesus cried out with a loud voice—John says it was a cry of overcoming—and died.

At another level, according to Matthew, there were significant occurrences in nature. The sun was darkened from noon until three o'clock. There was an earthquake, and the curtain between the temple court and the Holy of Holies was ripped in two. The earthquake also opened many tombs, and dead persons came forth to walk through the city as predicted by Daniel 12:2. And the centurion and his men guarding Jesus were astonished and believed that he was indeed the Son of God.

The phrase in verse 53, "after his resurrection," suggests that this entire paragraph (verses 51–54) is out of sequence here, and really belongs after the resurrection. This would agree with the fact that Pilate appointed soldiers to guard the tomb of Jesus. But Mark, who does not mention the supernatural occurrences, says that the centurion confessed that Jesus was the Son of God when he watched him breathe his last on the cross.

Ernest Hemingway, the famous novelist, once wrote a brief play called *Today Is Friday*. It consists entirely of the conversation of two soldiers in a bar on the afternoon following the crucifixion. One line is repeated again and again. "He was good in there today," they say. "He was good in there today." It is the central impression made by the man on the middle cross. However confusing the record may be in other respects—about what actually happened at the cross and what at the tomb—there is no doubt about this. He died with faith and dignity. "He was good in there today."

It is an interesting and somewhat pathetic footnote that the women who had followed Jesus all the way from Galilee watched the grim proceedings from a distance. In their society they were all but powerless to intervene. We can only hope that if the priesthood and Sanhedrin had been open to female membership, mercy might have tempered the decisions reached by the men.

> *Lord, I am trying to recall the most terrible pain I have ever felt. It made me cry at the time. Remembering it now makes the suffering of Jesus more real. What a horrible death it was. How helpless the women must have felt as they watched! But what a miracle, Lord! That one death has been more curative of sick humanity than all the music ever played, all the gardens ever visited, and all the laws ever enacted! I can only thank you in the name of him who suffered. Amen.*

Week XII: Wednesday

27:57–66 LAID IN A BORROWED TOMB

Joseph, according to the other Gospels, was a member of the Council of Elders (Mark 15:43) and did not give his consent to Jesus' death (Luke 23:50–51). If he was already a disciple at the time of Jesus' trial, it is possible that the meeting of the Council was called hastily and with only a select membership present. John 19:38–39 says that Joseph's relationship to Jesus was secret, and indicates that Nicodemus helped him remove the body and inter it.

Secret or not, it surely required considerable courage and devotion of Joseph to go to Pilate and request the body. Whether the disciples and the women lacked courage to do the same is beside the point; as strangers to the city, they would have had no place to bury Jesus, and a criminal's body was considered a defilement, especially on the Sabbath, which was almost upon them. At least the two Marys did not hesitate to be identified with Jesus, and came to mourn by the tomb.

We can only wonder what was really in the minds of the priests and Pharisees in requesting a guard for the tomb. Were they actually afraid of theft, or was it more than that they feared?

> Lord, Jesus was laid in a borrowed crib when he was born and a borrowed tomb when he died. Truly he had no home, no place to lay his head. His life was a perfect example of the selflessness he preached. Now let him live in our hearts forever, for we owe him everything. Amen.

Week XII: Thursday

28:1–10 FALL DOWN AND WORSHIP!

This is the first instance we have of followers of Jesus other than the inner circle of disciples actually worshiping him. Before, they doubtless admired him, listened to him, puzzled over him, perhaps even loved him. But here Matthew says explicitly that the two Marys fell at his feet and worshiped. His resurrection identified him so completely with the power of God in establishing the new creation that the women did not hesitate to share with him the kind of adoration normally reserved for God the Father.

The four Gospels vary in the details of the resurrection narrative, but all are agreed on one thing: It was Mary Magdalene's devotion to Jesus that caused her to be at the tomb at daybreak on the first day of the week and led to her being the first of Jesus' followers to see him in his resurrected form.

Can it be then that love is the only prelude to true worship? It was love that kept Mary Magdalene near the cross in the hours of agony, that brought her to the sepulcher where Joseph and

Nicodemus buried Jesus, and that caused her to return at daybreak after the Sabbath. And it was love's vision of the risen Christ that led her to fall down to worship him.

Here was a perfect example of Jesus' teachings about the Kingdom of God. The scribes and Pharisees kept the Law with rigorous devotion. But that was not enough. Our righteousness must exceed that of the scribes and Pharisees, said Jesus—it must be characterized by love and forgiveness and joy. And Mary embodied the faith of the new order, because she loved so much.

> Lord, how these women's lives must have been transformed from the events of Friday, when they watched from afar the gruesome execution of Jesus, to this remarkable Sunday morning in the garden where the tomb was. They were no longer on the periphery of things, helpless onlookers in a tragic drama; now they were at the center, touching the feet of the risen Lord, being sent to tell the others where to find him. Help us all to move from the one experience to the other. Let us fall down and worship because something extraordinary has happened to us. Through Jesus, who has been glorified through the resurrection. Amen.

Week XII: Friday

28:11–15 THE SOLDIERS TAKE A BRIBE

We can only be saddened by the guards' response to the miracle they had witnessed. How typical it is of people of every age. They had been present at the most wonderful event in history, yet resolved to treat it as a mere opportunity to make some cash and go on living as they had before.

Most of us, like these soldiers, regularly pass up chances to enter new dimensions of existence. We are so bent on earning a living or achieving status that we never even see the potential of great moments when they come to us. We miss the Kingdom that is in our midst, and fail to realize that the new creation waits at our very door to be born.

> Lord, if I were only waiting at the tomb like the women, instead of rushing around trying to make a better living like the soldiers, you would appear to me more often. Save me, I pray, from my own spiritual sloth. Through Jesus, who is the Christ. Amen.

Week XII: Saturday

28:16–20 THE NEW AGE OF THE SPIRIT

Matthew must have been running out of papyrus when he neared the end of his Gospel, for he condensed so much in this brief paragraph.

Jesus meets the eleven disciples, as is consistent with Matthew's emphasis throughout on his role as leader of the disciples, at a mountain in Galilee. We recall too the significance of mountains in the Gospel—especially the Sermon on the Mount and the Mount of Transfiguration. It is fitting that the one who is greater than Moses should give his final instructions from the mountain.

"By whose authority do you do these things?" the scribes and Pharisees had asked him. Now he says, "All authority in heaven and on earth has been given to me." The verb is perfect tense—it has already been accomplished. The disciples are to go to all the nations, as the coming of the magi and the healing of the Canaanite woman's daughter had prefigured, and make followers of all who believe. The baptism with which they baptize is not visibly different from John's baptism to fulfill all righteousness; but now it is in the name of the Son too, and of the Holy Spirit, for all of this is in and of the Spirit.

The disciples, moreover, are to teach those they baptize. They are to instruct them in all the things Matthew has tried to set down in his Gospel. The Kingdom is not to be a mere charismatic movement, strong on emotion and weak in doctrine. It is to have a firm and dynamic ethical foundation, going beyond the mere legal righteousness of the scribes and Pharisees. The Law of God is to truly flourish in the world.

And the most marvelous thing of all—the secret of the age of the Spirit—is that Jesus is now released from being in only one place at a time. Now he can appear freely to any disciple in any location at any moment when he chooses to disclose himself, and he will make himself known wherever disciples meet in his name. The child born in Bethlehem has become Lord of all creation!

> *O Lord, who taught and healed and broke bread with the disciples, teach, heal, and break bread with us. Renew the sense of your presence among us, that your teachings may gain new purchase on our imaginations. Let us live as those who have seen the hope of the ages consummated and know that you are indeed the Christ, the Son of the living God; and let us go and make disciples as you have commanded. For yours is the Kingdom and the power and the glory forever. Amen.*

A Closer Look at the Author

I was born on a farm near the little community of Germantown, Kentucky, during the height of the Great Depression. My father, an out-of-work agricultural agent, lived with my mother in her parents' home and operated a peddler's wagon. The night I was born he forgot to cover his baby pheasants and they all froze. It was an inauspicious beginning to a generally happy and fortunate life.

I grew up as an extremely myopic boy in the small towns of Stanford, Cynthiana, and Somerset, Kentucky. I didn't know I could not see well and my eyes were not tested until I was almost ten years old. I think that living in a blurry world as I did had much to do with my becoming a mystic and a dreamer. Even after I had glasses, I loved to take them off and turn the world into a haze again, especially at Christmas, when the lights were bright and colorful.

My mother went to work outside the home when I was ten. My only sister was killed by a runaway truck when I was twelve. This aggravated a period of mid-life crisis for my parents, and they went through a time of difficult adjustment. I spent much time alone, working over my drawing board or taking long, meditative walks in the woods and along the creeks. It was there that the sense of God really began to develop in me. Later, Wordsworth was to be one of my favorite poets.

In the summer before my senior year in high school, shortly after I had turned sixteen, I felt a calling to the Christian ministry. Aborting my plans to become an artist, I joined the newly formed debate society in our school and soon enjoyed a modest success as a public speaker. A clergyman with whom I consulted advised me that Baylor University would be a most suitable college, inasmuch as I was going to become a Baptist minister. It was a long way off and I hadn't much money, but I believed that in God all things are possible, so I went down to Texas and enrolled.

At the end of my first year at Baylor it became necessary to return to Kentucky to earn more money. For a while, I sold Bibles and cookbooks, but was not enormously successful at that. When the pulpit of a rural Baptist church fell vacant, I asked for it and was soon ordained as a minister. For a year I attended classes at Georgetown College and commuted to the church field on the weekends. In addition to preaching twice each weekend, I courted the piano player and, at the end of the year, married her. Anne was seventeen then, and our wedding was on my nineteenth birthday. Three months later, we packed all of our belongings into a twelve-year-old Ford and set out for Texas, where I completed my B.A. degree at the end of the next academic year.

Feeling grossly immature and inadequate to undertake seminary training at my age, I decided to pursue graduate study in some field that would broaden my understanding of life. I had been much impressed by one of my English professors, so I enrolled at the University of Kentucky in the Department of English. I expected to take only a master's degree, but found the course so agreeable that I stayed four years and completed a doctor's degree as well. My thesis, which was written on the fiction of Ernest Hemingway, was later published by the University Press of Kentucky. One well-meaning professor, knowing that I intended to become a minister, or indeed already was, tried to steer me toward another subject; the writings of Jeremy Taylor, he was convinced, would be much more appropriate for clerical study. I have always been thankful that I did not follow that advice, for I learned much about both life and art from Hemingway.

During these four years I was pastor of a small church near Renfro Valley, Kentucky. It was on a dirt road, and during the spring rains we often had to drive very fast down the hills to get through the sloughs of soft mud in the bottoms. The pay was pitifully small, but the fellowship was always warm. If I have learned anything about human nature, it was mostly from the simple folk in my rural parishes; they disguised few of their basic emotions from me, and studying them was as profitable as reading the books required in school.

The next part of our pilgrimage took Anne and me to Massachusetts, where I entered the Divinity School at Harvard University and also became the minister of Martin's Pond Union Baptist Church in North Reading, a few miles north of Boston. Harvard was a feast of an experience to me with its great traditions, learned professors, and cosmopolitan environment. Anne busied herself with the piano, studying for two years with Miss Jeannette Giguere at the New England Conservatory. We lived in a delightful little parsonage above Martin's Pond—our first house—and reveled in the magnificent autumns and snowy New England winters.

Wishing to return to the South but having no connections for securing a pastorate there, I accepted a position as Assistant Professor of English at Georgetown College, where I had studied briefly as an undergraduate. We spent two wonderful years there. During the first, Anne taught on the music faculty, and in the second she bore our first son, John Eric. I had become the chapel preacher during the second year and was given the double honor of having the school yearbook dedicated to me for the quality of the chapel programs and being elected the most popular professor on the campus.

It was not a good time to leave, but Dr. Paul Scherer, the great Lutheran preacher and teacher, had recently gone to Princeton Theological Seminary to teach homiletics, and asked if I would come to study with him and be his associate. I went and had two rich years at Princeton, during which I pastored a small Baptist congregation in Edison, New Jersey, earned a doctor's degree in Homiletics and Liturgics, and wrote a book called *The Failure of Theology in Modern Literature*.

From Princeton, we moved to Louisville, Kentucky, where I became the academic dean of a new liberal arts college called Kentucky Southern. My principal duties were to help in the formation of an interdisciplinary curriculum and to secure the faculty to implement it. While we were in Louisville, our second son, Paul Krister, was born. As I began to receive queries about my interest in various college presidencies, I decided that I must leave Kentucky Southern College or be typed as a college administrator for the rest of my life. I wished much more to be a minister, so quickly accepted a position as Associate Professor of Preaching at Vanderbilt University's Divinity School when it was proffered.

At the time of this writing, I have been at Vanderbilt for twelve years. It has been a rich time in many ways. My students have been a constant source of stimulation to me; most of them have become good friends, and we continue to correspond through the years. I have had time to grow up with my sons, and have learned much from them. Our family spent a sabbatical year in Paris, France, and greatly benefited from the experience of another culture. Anne and I have walked and dreamed together, and have even written music together. We began by collaborating on a musical comedy about Zen Buddhism, then went on to write a number of hymns and anthems, some of which are presently in the stage of being published.

In many ways, I think I am still the nearsighted boy I was as I tracked the fields and creeks of Kentucky. I wear contact lenses now, and I travel all over the world, speaking to churches, universities, and military groups. But I still love to walk out of doors, and to find quiet places where I can reflect and be in touch with God. If there is any special quality this series of devotional commentaries possesses, I hope it will be that of mystical insight, gathered and distilled onto the pages in moments of thoughtful communion.

I am grateful for the opportunity to write the commentaries. I hope you find the use of them as meaningful to you as the composition of them is gratifying to me. The Bible is a remarkable book, a very special book, and I cannot but feel a thrill at the prospect of having this work laid out before me for years to come.